P9-DMW-525

From Teens to Marriage

From

TEENS

To

MARRIAGE

By

REUBEN D. BEHLMER

CONCORDIA PUBLISHING HOUSE • SAINT LOUIS

The Library of Congress has cataloged this book as follows:

Behlmer, Reuben D
    From teens to marriage. Saint Louis, Concordia Pub.
House [c1959]
    112 p.   22cm.

    1. Sex.   2. Marriage.   I. Title.

HQ35.B4   *301.426   392.5   58–9440 ‡

Library of Congress   5

Dear Teen-Ager:

You are one of many millions of young people between the ages of thirteen and twenty. Yours is an age unlike any other time of life. You are beyond childhood but have not yet reached the full state of maturity. During these years you will experience tremendous changes in body maturity, interests, and outlook on life. The world looks wonderful one day, and the next day it seems frightening. You feel you cannot grow up fast enough. You have parents, teachers, and friends continually advising you as to what and what not to do. You may fall in love once or many times; or, on the other hand, love may elude you completely. In your later teens you will graduate from high school and make plans to attend college, or you may get a job and begin making your bid as a successful employee. Society feels you are not old enough to vote and have a voice in government, yet your physical maturity and stamina are recognized as being capable of fulfilling all the demands of exacting and sometimes strenuous military service.

Temptations are many. Your sex instincts urge you to experience the privileges of married life; but you have been taught, and you know, that sex relations before marriage are wrong. How to meet this challenge is not easy. You may become associated with a group at school or at work who feel that life is dull. They want a thrill now and then. Some look for it in drinking, while others try to find it in the power which is theirs under the hood of a late-model automobile. Your church has taught you to know the Bible and the way you should live. It has taught you how to follow the teachings of Christ and to be an influence for good. You know your talents, but the question is how and where to use them correctly. You will be challenged many times to take the path of least resistance or to follow the crowd that has convictions contrary to your own. You have the power to choose right from wrong. This power of choice is a tremendous responsibility, for on it depends the future. You not only are the hope of the future, but you are the future. In a few short years you will be an adult taking the place of those who are now in positions of leadership. You have no alternative but to make a choice; it will either be for a life of happiness, service, and accomplishments, or one of disappointments, failures, and regrets.

It is the sincere wish of the author that this book will aid you to become the kind of adult that God and your parents and friends wish you to be — a man or woman Christian in character, successful in educational attainments and social maturity — and in due time to establish a home in which love and devotion prevail.   REUBEN D. BEHLMER

CONTENTS

Introduction

CHAPTER ONE

You and Your Wonderful Body   1
Home   3
Brothers and Sisters   5
Independence   6
Friends   6
School   7
Religion   9
Problems   11
The Future   12

CHAPTER TWO

Who Am I?   13
Heredity   14
Personality   16

CHAPTER THREE

The Story of Life and Reproduction   17
The Female Reproductive System   19
The Male Reproductive System   21
Conception, Development, and Birth of a Baby   23
Correlative Information   27
Growing into Maturity   33
Dating   36
Love   60
Thinking It Through   68
Now We Are Engaged   75
Mixed Marriages   81
Early Marriages   90
The Marriage Ceremony   96
The Honeymoon   99
What Married Life Means   101
Conclusion   109
What to Read   110

CHAPTER ONE

You and Your Wonderful Body

You have been wonderfully made by the divine Creator. (Psalm 139:14.) Your body is the most complex and wonderful thing of all creation. Its cells have the ability to grow, repair, and reproduce with no conscious effort on your part. Your body wages heroic battles with disease and infections. Your heart, no larger than your fist, pumps tons of blood through thousands of miles of blood vessels daily. Millions of messages are relayed to and from your brain. Nothing that man has created equals your brain with its ability of creative thought and the memory of things you have seen and heard. No blessing of God is greater than a healthy body and mind; yet the responsibility for its care and use rests squarely on you. An excellent rule to follow for good health and physical efficiency is "moderation." Lack of rest and overindulgence in eating, drinking, smoking, etc., lead to decreased efficiency and broken health. NO ONE has ever cheated on his body for any length of time and come out the winner. You have but ONE body and ONE life; do not waste it.

It is interesting to note that all parts of your body work in full co-operation and in harmony with each other. This is especially true of the complete integration of mind and body. Man was created superior to the animals in that he was given a brain with the marvelous faculty of reason. Your brain is uniquely different from an animal's brain in that it has a center which gives you the power of judgment, the power not only to determine what to eat and wear but to discern right from wrong. Your so-called conscience is a part of this center. It is a type of warning signal which flashes red, so to speak, when you do wrong. Like other warning signals, it becomes unreliable when ignored or misused. When it is deliberately ignored for a period of time, its signals become weak and scarcely noticeable.

Few people inherit a brain incapable of achieving exceptional things if the spirit of work and application are used for its development. The splitting of the atom and its adaptation to modern use is ample proof. The seemingly unlimited potential of the brain may lead one to the supposition that all things can be governed and overcome through the power of the will and the intellect. As we marvel at the mind and body of man, it must be recognized that they are the creation of God, and only to the extent that we remain in harmony with the laws of nature and the will of our Creator can we reflect the best that is in us.

Home

A person is the product of many influences; one of the most important is the home — your home. What does "home" mean to you? How do you feel toward your father, mother, brothers, and sisters? In all probability you have parents who love you, understand you, and are sympathetic toward you. If this be true, you enjoy your home. From this pleasant experience you learn the formula for establishing your own home when the time comes.

Not all homes experience success in personal relationships. Quarreling between father and mother, or between parents and children, creates a feeling of insecurity and frustration for all the family. This lack of harmony may affect the way the home is kept and managed. If it is your misfortune to come from a home of this type, it does not necessarily follow that you cannot establish a successful home of your own. It does mean, however, that it will require careful analysis, study, and prayerful determination to build a happy home of your own. You have one advantage, for you have experienced what disharmony can do in a family. Surely, you will be willing to pay the price for success in your own home.

Unfortunately, many young people feel their parents are old-fashioned and do not understand the younger generation. It might be true that your parents are old-fashioned in their ideas, and in what they will or will not let you do. However, this does not mean they do not love you or care for you. It is YOUR responsibility to try to understand them. Your parents are human and may have been influenced by environments and circumstances far different from yours. This

3

is not to mean that twenty-five or thirty years ago the things your parents learned and did were wrong, or that only the present way is right. The principle of right and wrong does not change. Its application to modern times and circumstances might change. As an example, stealing and lying have always been wrong and always will be. Your parents understand this and so do you. It may be, however, that your parents do not understand the extent to which the social life of young people has changed since they were your age. Coming in from a date at eleven o'clock may seem late to them; but to you one o'clock may seem quite reasonable. Your parents are more modern than you suppose, if you honestly try to understand them. To teen-agers, parents do not always make sense in what they say, do, and expect. But when the twenties are reached, enough maturity has been acquired so that the interests and wishes of parents are better understood. Mother and father may not know the latest song hits, or the latest style of clothes, but you will find their ideas and advice sound and to your best interest. They do make mistakes, for they are human. Nothing is gained in a home by exchanging "an eye for an eye and a tooth for a tooth." Happiness is more abundant when all in a family are tolerant and learn to give and take. Family freedom, like any freedom, is freedom only when the rights and privileges of others are respected.

When mother and father are mistaken, what can and should you do? A friendly discussion and an understanding approach are certainly in order; only too often this is not done. What good can come from angry, insulting remarks, pouting, or quarreling? The Bible gives this direction to children: "Honor thy father and thy mother" (Deuteronomy 5:16). This implies respect for their authority and judgment, and appreciation of the many sacrifices they have made for you. The years in which you, as a teen-age child, will be at home with your parents are fast slipping away. Do nothing that will cause regret in the years to come. A point temporarily gained is not worth years of regret. No hurt is felt more deeply by parents than wounds caused by their children. Consider it a privilege to act in a manner pleasing to your parents and to do the things that will make them proud of you. Making them unhappy will not add to your happiness. When you are married and have children of your own, the interest of your parents will then be fully appreciated. Do unto your parents as you would have them do unto you. A commercial on television would say, "Try it and see the difference."

Brothers and Sisters

Brothers and sisters normally love one another; however, they also quarrel. Much of their disagreement stems from a difference of sex and maturity. Young adults want to feel mature and independent. Your younger brothers or sisters want to do things which seem childish to you; the things they do annoy you. Remember, you, too, were once not understood by older brothers or sisters. Tolerance and understanding is not a natural trait; it must be cultivated. You are a part of your family, and your help and guidance is needed along with that of mother and father to make your family life a happy one. In a few short years younger brothers and sisters will grow up.

You will then look back with satisfaction and pride to know that your guidance and help was a factor in their success.

Independence

What is independence, and how can it be acquired? As a teen-ager you probably feel you should be independent, permitted the freedom of making your own decisions, and doing with your time and money as you choose. Independence is something every young person looks forward to; but it does not come by instinct, like the speed and sureness with which a young bird learns to fly. Independence is not acquired automatically; it must be learned and earned. The measure of independence that will be granted you depends on the maturity you demonstrate.

Friends

What is a friend? How many friends should you have? Where can they be found? The selection of friends is one of your major responsibilities. You are judged by the friends you have. There is truth in the expression, "Birds of a feather flock together." You want to be proud of your friends, proud of the way they talk, proud of their interests and their character. These qualities are much more important than their social rating. To have a good social rating is commendable, but not at the sacrifice of stability and character. Your need for choosing friends is continuous throughout life, be it in school, church, place of work, or in organizations to which you may belong. A logical question to ask is, By what yardstick can friends or potential friends be measured? How can they be evaluated? One requisite of a friend is that he share your ideals and interests. Of course, there must be affection, too. A person who shows no special interest in you is hardly a friend. One true test of friendship is the readiness with which your friends will come to your assistance in time of need and trouble. A friend need not and should not always agree with you. In fact, a good friend will be frank with you concerning wrong habits, errors in judgment, or whatever else injures your welfare.

School

Mentioning school is a thrill to some teen-agers and a bore to others. In any case, your school life rivals your home life in the influence it has on you. It presents an opportunity for development that is limited only by your own limitations. The author asked a class of high school seniors this question: "If you had your high school career to live over again, what would you do differently than you have done?" Two major opinions were expressed: (1) Study harder and get better grades. (2) Take part in more school functions. The first of these speaks for itself. Achievement in schoolwork can be had only for a price; that price is study. You may have the capacity to learn, but knowledge is something that must be acquired. There are no short cuts to knowledge; its foundation is hard work and a desire to achieve. School is fun when you do your work well and get good grades because

YOU want to. It is boresome if you feel that you complete your assignments to please the teacher or to earn a barely passing grade. The subjects required are for your good, not just something to fill up your schedule. Teachers are glad to help and guide you; but if you ignore their offer of assistance, there is little they can do. School is similar to a hot-rod automobile. The more time and effort you devote to making it attractive and keeping the motor properly tuned, the better it will perform and the more pleasure you will derive from it. School is like that, too, for you receive in direct proportion to what you give. Going to school is a full-time job. Your parents, teachers, and the thousands of citizens who pay taxes expect you to do your best. They know the need of an education and what it will mean to you. In a sense, it is stealing if you squander your opportunities and talents on a good time; for opportunities lost and talents wasted can never be regained. Your educational record has meaning. Many times in the future your school will be asked to give your record of achievement to a pro-spective employer. It will give you real satisfaction to know that the school principal can write good and praiseworthy things about your attendance, conduct, and scholastic achievement.

Of course, school is not only for academic achieve-ment. Every school offers opportunities through extra-curricular activities to meet new friends and enrich social experiences. Athletics, clubs, parties, plays, etc., offer much enjoyment and opportunity to make new friends. Some students go to the extreme and become too active in these affairs. When this occurs, energy and talents are spread over so many areas that more is lost than gained. It may be that your talents and interests do not lie in athletics or school clubs. This does not mean that you cannot take part in school functions, for there are numerous "service" opportunities, such as clerical assistants, messengers, athletic team managers, etc. These opportunities must be sought; nothing will come to you without some effort on your part.

Learning how to get along with teachers and make new school friends is as much a part of education as is history and English. A simple test of your friendliness and ability to make friends can be found in the school cafeteria, corridors, and classrooms. Do you have friends with whom you eat, thereby making the lunch period fun and relaxation? Or does your lunch period consist of a ten-minute process of devouring food by yourself, then rushing from the cafeteria, again to be alone in your dream world? Are you greeted in the corridors or on the campus by fellow students? When the school office or a teacher wants something done which lies in your ability, have you made yourself well enough known that they will think of you to do the job? School presents unlimited opportunities in acquiring an academic education, developing leadership, and making friends. Do not let opportunity pass you by.

Religion

Few people actually profess that they do not believe in God or do not have a religious belief of some sort. Religion to you may mean doing no wrong and being charitable with your time and money. On the other hand, it may mean all these things plus something much more fundamental — the conviction that a belief in Jesus Christ as your Savior and Guide is necessary for a happy life.

The kind of religion you have and the way you practice it will, in a large measure, follow the teaching and beliefs of your home. A home where father, mother, and children worship together will have an emphasis and influence different from the home where interest on Sunday lies in doing the family wash, gardening, or catching up on sleep lost the night before. To be religious does not mean you must live an abnormal life and not have fun. It does mean, however, that what you say and do comes within the framework of the teachings of the Bible. Doing wrong, evading the law, transgressing the Commandments is not the fun some suppose it to be. Your purpose in life should be to serve God and your fellow men, be an influence for good in all you say and do, use your talents to the best interest of society and self, and to know Jesus Christ as "the Way, the Truth, and the Life."

As a teen-ager you make many choices and decisions of your own. This is as it should be. The choice concerning religion is also yours; you can accept it or reject it. God forces no one to follow Him. He has given you a brain for thinking and reasoning. Intelligence, education, and reason sometimes seem to be the only logical and sensible solutions to our problems, yet without faith we will fail. Faith is of the Spirit, a fifth dimension known only to those who experience its power. Faith, says the Bible, is "the substance of things hoped for, the evidence of things not seen" (Hebrews 11:1). Life is largely a matter of following routines in daily living. If, in these routines, a few minutes are set aside each day for prayer and meditation, you will not only be following God's wish, but the experience of communion with God will be a source of spiritual, mental, and physical relaxation and strength. Being religious is not being weak; it often takes courage. You have your choice — which will it be?

Problems

It is normal for all young people to have problems. People of all ages have problems, but they vary as to kind, seriousness, and complexity. Difficulties and hardships are essential for growth and achievement. The athlete who does not train beyond the point of what will be required of him in competition will be beaten by the athlete who has paid the price of rigid training and self-discipline. Living is a type of athletic contest, and to meet the challenge we must be in training. The better we have trained ourselves, the more able we will be to meet our problems. Our chief concern should be how we will solve our problems when they come — and come they will.

The world is beset with problems that test the very limit of a person's capacity to get along with his fellow beings. You, as a teen-ager, must share some of these problems. But of more immediate and vital concern to you personally are the problems of young people that revolve around their relationship to the social order. Some problems that confront the teen-ager are: Should or should I not have my own automobile? How can I get my parents to see I am growing up and should be given more freedom? Is it better to go steady, or to date many different boys or girls, as the case may be? Is it necessary to pet in order to be popular? How can I meet the problem of money which is needed for the activities of teen-age life? The list could be extended. All problems must be met forthrightly and with courage. No escape mechanism will satisfactorily solve a problem. One test of maturity is the ability to solve problems. There is no alternative; you must find solutions to your problems in a way which is acceptable to society, the laws of the land, and your Christian principles.

The Future

The future is yours to wonder, hope, and dream about. What you wish for your future depends largely upon your age, sex, ambitions, and economic background. You have much to look forward to. Furthering your education, finding a job, making new friends, marriage, and the rearing of a family are just a few of the experiences in the forward look. The future will contain both success and failure. But it can be a bright future if you face each situation squarely, with faith in God and the best that is in you. The will to succeed and confidence in your own abilities are ingredients of success.

In the following chapter we shall analyze who you are, and why you are what you are.

CHAPTER TWO

Who Am I?

Have you ever stopped to ask yourself, Who am I? It seems absurd, doesn't it? A person should know who he is. The fact is, however, many people do not know; they have never analyzed themselves. A study of oneself is not only interesting but also essential for a successful career, marriage, and social adjustment.

It is interesting to note that there is no other person in the world like you — there never has been, and there never will be. This in itself should make you feel your importance and worth. What would life be like if God had seen fit to create all humans alike in appearance and abilities? Under such circumstances living would indeed be monotonous and unchallenging. For example: It would be impossible to have fun and interest in competitive athletics because one team would have no more ability than the other. Imagine what would happen if you attended a social function and others looked and acted just like you; if everyone in school would get the same grades and do the same things, and if you could not distinguish your history teacher from your English teacher. These illustrations are enough to show the absurdity of it all. You should be grateful that you are an individual different from all others, a person with a physique, personality, and ability you can call your own. Understanding yourself is essential to achieving success in life, whether it be in school, business, or marriage. For this study of yourself let us begin with heredity.

Heredity

When God created the world, he made it to be governed by fundamental truths called laws of nature. Scientists have been seriously probing into these truths of nature for centuries. Some of their most recent achievements are: harnessing the atom, discovery of antibiotics, the invention of television. All of these were here on earth for discovery since the time of creation, but not until recently has man been able to piece together the laws and powers of nature as expressed in the tremendous advancement of science. Man-made satellites are circling the earth. Trips to the moon and other planets will soon be a reality. The satellite Telstar has demonstrated that television on an international basis is here.

As the atom is a part of this well-designed and well-regulated universe, so is your body a miracle of living matter. Your body is not a chance collection of cells, organs, and systems, but a well-organized and functioning unit. One of the most amazing of its functions is performed by the sex or reproductive cell.

14

These cells, produced by the testes in men, are called sperms; those produced by the ovaries in women are called eggs or ova. You, like all other human beings, were created by the union of a sperm from your father and an egg or ovum from your mother. Sperm and ovum are very complex cells. Both kinds carry chromosomes and genes, the elements which transmit characteristics. The human cell has forty-eight chromosomes, twenty-four from the mother and twenty-four from the father. No other form of life has the same kind of chromosomes as the human being. Young people frequently ask why brothers and sisters differ in looks and in many other ways, since they come from the same parents. This is another miracle of nature. Of the hundreds of millions of sperms produced by each male during his lifetime, no two are alike, and of the thousands of ova produced by a woman no two are alike. It must follow that since the union of a particular sperm and egg cannot be duplicated, no two people can be alike. An exception to this law is in the case of identical twins; here the egg divides to form two embryos. Only one sperm can fertilize an egg, and when that egg divides, both of the embryos must have the same formula of chromosomes as the original sperm and egg. The usual pattern is for the egg not to divide; hence an individual embryo is formed and a single birth takes place, giving life to a person unlike anyone in the past, present, or future.

Your hereditary characteristics are inherited from all of your ancestors, but those of your parents and grandparents are the most dominant. You will find in yourself physical and mental traits which are also dominant in them. You can understand yourself better when you understand them and their influence on you.

Personality

Your personality is the sum total of many influencing factors. You were not born with a ready-made personality; it must be acquired. Every experience and influence in your life contributes in some way to making you the kind of person you are. It will make a difference whether you are born of wealthy parents or of those of moderate means; they will do things differently and their influence on you will be different. If your background is of German descent, the concept of the way children should be reared and disciplined will be different from what it would be if, for example, you were of French extraction. The kind of religion you have and the degree with which you practice it, influences you as a person. Good health influences differently than does poor health. If you come from a home where father and mother love each other and their children, its influence on you will certainly be different from that of a home where quarreling prevails or a home which has been broken by divorce.

It becomes increasingly clear that what we are stems from the influencing factors of heredity and environment. Interests, abilities, ideals, attitudes, and ambitions all have their influence on you. As you grow older you will change somewhat; but the pattern of life you have established by the time you graduate from high school will not vary much in its basic elements. Knowing and appreciating your own influences will aid in knowing and appreciating those of others. Before long you will be considering marriage and the selection of a marriage partner. It is essential to marital success to know your marriage partner well.

CHAPTER THREE

The Story of Life and Reproduction

Knowing the process of birth, as well as the structure and functions of the reproductive organs, will lead us to appreciate the miracle and dignity of that which God has created and man so frequently disgraces. In school you have studied the care and functions of the body. But unless you took an advanced science or health course, it is not very probable that you have thoroughly studied the reproductive system. In this discussion we wish to deal with the reproductive system with the same frankness and thoroughness that we would give the skeletal, vascular, nervous, muscular, digestive, or respiratory systems. The reproductive system is an integral part of the body; it is that just as much as the other systems mentioned. There is nothing "dirty" or vulgar about either the reproductive system or the study of it. As mentioned before, it is a system created by God, the same as all other systems of the body. The reproductive organs are neither good nor bad from a moral point of view; their function is to produce the cells for the propagation of the human race. Sex and the reproductive system become a moral issue only when they are used wrongly in the sight of God and contrary to the laws of the land. Also other systems of the body can be abused and misused so as to become moral issues. To illustrate: Excessive drinking dulls the mind and slows the nervous reflexes, thereby making a potential killer out of an intoxicated driver of an automobile. From this we would not assume that there is something bad or wrong about one's nervous system. It was, however, abused. Man's ability to think and reason gives him the power of doing with his body what he chooses. In the bonds of marriage, sex can be used in a spirit of love and esteem. However, sex can also be used in a degrading and sinful way by the married or unmarried. The choice is ours to make.

To understand sex in its entirety a knowledge of the structure and function of the reproductive organs is essential. This knowledge may not make you more moral, but it will give you an understanding that can be acquired in no other way. On pages 19—23 the individual parts of the male and female reproductive systems are listed and briefly explained. Note in particular the scientific names used. These are the same names as those used by the medical profession; and these you need not hesitate to use. Doctors and scientists use them with frankness and in a dignified manner. The common street variety of names has no place in the teaching and discussion of this system.

The Female Reproductive System

1. The external genitalia, or vulva

   a. Mons pubis

   The most prominent portion of the external genitalia is known as the *mons pubis*.

   b. Outer labia

   The word "labia" means lips. The outer labia are on each side of the vagina, and their outer surface is partly covered with hair.

   c. Inner labia

   Two small lips concealed by the outer labia.

   d. Clitoris

   A small cylindrical organ similar to the penis of the male. The clitoris is composed of erectile tissue and is essentially a sense organ. It is located at the front of the inner labia.

   e. Urethra

   Strictly speaking, the urethra is not a part of the reproductive system, but it is considered as part of the vulva. The urethra is a tube or duct which leads from the urinary bladder to the exterior of the body.

   f. Hymen

   The hymen is a thin membrane covering the opening of the vagina. The popular concept that if it is broken before marriage the woman is not a virgin, is not necessarily true.

It might be broken in the active life of the modern girl.

2. Internal female organs

The female pelvis is broad and shallow as contrasted with the deep and narrow male pelvis. The genital organs housed in the female pelvis are:

a. Vagina

The vagina, which is also sometimes referred to as the birth canal, receives the penis of the male during sex relations. During the process of birth it stretches to the extent of allowing for the passage of the baby.

b. Uterus

The uterus, or womb, as it is also called, is a pear-shaped organ approximately two and one-half to three inches in length and two inches in width. At the opening is the cervix, which extends somewhat into the upper end of the vagina. The uterus is held in place by round ligaments and other supporting tissues. The position of the uterus is important. If it is tilted too far forward or backward, the passage of the sperms might be blocked; this may cause infertility.

c. Fallopian tubes (oviducts)

The Fallopian tubes are approximately four inches in length and are supported by a broad ligament. One end of each tube is attached to the uterus; the other end is funnel-shaped and has fingerlike projections called fimbriae. The function of the tube is to carry the matured ovum or egg to the uterus. If sperms are present in the Fallopian tube at the time an ovum is present, fertilization of the ovum is likely to occur.

d. Ovaries

The ovaries are two almond-shaped bodies approximately one and one-half inches in length. They lie deep in the lower pelvis, one on each side. The ovaries have two important functions: (1) the production of the female germ cells known as ova; (2) the secretion of two female hormones: estrogen and progesterone. These hormones control the femininity of the individual and cause changes in the uterus during the menstrual cycle and pregnancy.

The Male Reproductive System

1. External male genitalia

a. Penis

The penis is a cylindrical organ composed of erectile tissue. This tissue is capable of becoming greatly distended with blood. When this occurs, the organ is in a state of erection, which is necessary for sex relations. The penis serves as a dual passageway for semen from the reproductive organs and for urine from the bladder.

b. Testes

The testes, or male sex glands, are two oval-shaped bodies approximately one and one-half inches long. Their function is the production of sperms, the male reproductive cells, and the production of a hormone called androgen. This hormone gives the male his secondary sex characteristics, such as deep voice, beard, and general body build.

c. Epididymis

The epididymis is a duct composed of some twenty smaller ducts that emerge from the testis and carry sperms from the testis.

d. Scrotum

The testes are contained in a pouch called the scrotum. Men, as well as male mammals, have the testes externally rather than internally. The testes of the fetus are formed in the abdominal cavity and descend through the inguinal canal into the scrotum about the time of birth.

2. Internal male genitalia

a. Vas deferens (sperm duct)

The vas deferens is a continuation of the epididymis. It passes into the body through the inguinal canal. From here it continues in the abdomen until it reaches the prostate gland. Each inguinal canal has a ring of strong fibrous tissue on its extremity. Normally these rings are closed and fit closely around the vasa deferentia. In some males the inguinal ring is too large, thus creating the possibility of an inguinal hernia (rupture).

b. Seminal vesicles

The seminal vesicles are two pouches connected to the *vas deferens*. The one pouch lies to the right and the other to the left of the midline of the bladder. They secrete a fluid which is a part of semen.

c. Prostate gland

The prostate gland is about the size of a walnut. It lies at the base of the urinary bladder. Its function is to contribute part of the fluid found in semen. Secretion of the prostate also stimulates the sperms to activity after being released.

d. Semen

Semen is a fluid discharged by the male during sexual stimulation. It is composed of sperms, which are produced in the testes, and of secretions from the prostate and other glands. Its discharge from the body is called ejaculation. The necessity for semen is readily understood. Sperms have the power of motion by means of a long tail which propels them forward. Sperms must go to meet the egg if fertilization of the egg is to take place. Semen is the medium in which sperms swim to reach the egg in the Fallopian tube.

Conception, Development, and Birth of a Baby

Marriage brings with it not only the desire of husband and wife to love and be loved, but also the desire to have children. Creating new life is a grand, God-given accomplishment of man and wife. Their children are the product of the two of them — physically, mentally, and spiritually. The more the true facts of conception and the development of the baby are understood, the more convincing is the fact that a miracle is performed with each birth.

During coitus (sexual intercourse) the male deposits sperms in the vagina near the cervix of the uterus. Sperms released in the vagina make their way into the uterus and on into the Fallopian tube. If an ovum, or female germ cell, is in the tube, one — and only one — of the millions of sperms released by the male will fertilize it. Fertilization occurs when the sperm enters the egg. At that very moment conception takes place, and the woman is pregnant. No more eggs will be produced by the ovary, and menstruation ceases until after the birth of the baby. After birth, the body returns to its normal shape and the natural cycle of ovulation and menstruation is resumed.

When the sperm enters the egg, new life is on its way. The fertilized egg then begins to multiply by dividing into two, four, eight, sixteen, thirty-two, etc., cells. The word "embryo" is used to designate this new life until the third month after conception. In three to ten days after conception, the embryo travels from the Fallopian tube to the uterus, where it develops and grows. In this early development the placenta, which is the organ connecting the baby and mother, functions to supply food from the mother to the baby and transfer waste from the baby to the mother. It connects with the baby through the umbilical cord.

The rate of growth after conception takes place is very rapid. By the end of the embryonic period the general body form is well developed; the eyes and ears

24

are beginning to appear; blood vessels are present, but not in their final form; the heart is developed enough to form its chambers and valves; and the testes in the male and the ovaries in the female are recognizable. The baby is well protected from injury as it lies suspended in a fluid-filled structure called the amniotic sac.

From the third month until birth the term "fetus" is used for the developing child. In the third month the fetus is approximately three inches long and begins to resemble a human. The head, however, is much larger in proportion to the rest of the body, and the temporary teeth are forming beneath the gums. In the fourth month the bones are outlined, and the uterus and vagina are recognizable in the female. In the male the testes are ready to begin their descent into the scrotum. The mother may detect the first bit of movement like a light fluttering of wings. In the fifth month the doctor is able to detect movements of the fetus when examining the mother's abdomen. By five or six months the fetus is about twelve inches long and has much the same appearance as at birth. The ability of a baby to live when born at seven months depends upon the degree to which the nervous system has developed. The last three months are a period of more detailed growth, with the whole body assuming the development necessary to live in the outside world. At birth, an average baby weighs about seven pounds and is approximately eighteen to twenty inches long.

The normal position of the baby in the uterus is head down, with arms and legs folded close to the body. In the last weeks before birth, the head is against the cervix of the uterus. Usually babies are born in this normal position, but in a small per cent of births other parts of the body appear first. The doctor determines the position of the child before delivery, and he is then prepared to make delivery as safe and easy as possible.

When the baby has reached full maturity, it is ready to be born. Birth is accomplished by a process called "labor." Labor consists of a series of contractions of the uterus and other muscles of the abdomen to force the baby downward and outward. These muscular contractions are infrequent at first, but as labor progresses, they become more frequent and intense. When labor pains begin to occur at frequent intervals, it is time to go to the hospital for delivery. The doctor will have advised the expectant mother as to the symptoms and progress of labor.

Labor occurs in several stages. In the first stage the cervix begins to dilate as the head of the infant descends into the birth canal. The length of this stage varies but is completed when the cervix (birth canal) is entirely dilated. The second stage of labor is more intense. The uterine muscles produce a bearing-down feeling, and the pains become more frequent. The descent of the baby through the birth canal is due to the force of the uterine contractions, which cause the child to move forward and finally emerge from the vagina. This action terminates the second stage of labor. The doctor assists with the birth in any way necessary. When the child is born, the doctor ties and cuts the umbilical cord a short distance from the baby's body. The end next to the body heals, forming the navel. The third stage of labor occurs after the child is born. The placenta is no longer of use and is expelled from the body. It is now referred to as the "afterbirth." The expelling of the afterbirth requires but a few minutes and brings to a close the third stage of labor.

A small per cent of women have birth passages too small to allow the baby to pass through normally. In this case, the doctor may decide to deliver the baby by surgery; this is called a Caesarean birth. Children delivered in this way have a normal chance of survival and growth.

A fetus born before completing the full term of nine months is known as a premature baby. If the baby is mature enough at the time of birth, it has a good chance to survive and develop into a normal child. A premature baby needs special care, usually in a hospital. It is placed in an incubator, a criblike machine which provides the same even temperature as the mother's body.

Correlative Information

Signs of Pregnancy

No one symptom should be taken as a positive sign of pregnancy, but any one, or a combination of signs, would indicate a woman should go to a doctor for confirmation. Following are some signs which might indicate pregnancy:

1. Cessation of menstruation is an early and important sign.

2. Morning sickness. Two out of three pregnant women experience some degree of nausea in the morning.

3. Frequent urination. This is caused by the pressure of the uterus against the bladder.

4. Change in breasts. The nipples become darker, and the breast may feel full and tender.

Time of Birth

No definite day and possibly not even the exact week for a given birth can be predicted. Full development of the human fetus is two hundred eighty days, more or less. The following rule is commonly used to determine the approximate time of delivery: Ascertain the first day of the last menstruation, add seven days, and count ahead nine months.

Interesting Information on Sperms

1. The sperm is the smallest cell in the human body. It is about one third the length of the ovum. It has a head, which contains the nucleus, and a long tail for locomotion.

2. The sperm is the only cell in the body which is able to travel under its own power.

3. The average man produces around 400,000 billion sperms during his lifetime.

4. 400 to 500 million spermatozoa are released at each discharge of semen.

5. Illness accompanied by high fever causes temporary infertility of the male.

6. If an older man is able to produce sperm cells strong and healthy enough to reach the ovum and fertilization occurs, the child of this man will have no adverse hereditary effects because of age. In other words, changes in body cells do not produce changes in sex cells.

Sex Determination

The male produces two kinds of sperm: an X sperm and a Y sperm. The female produces only an X-type egg. The male sperm determines whether the baby will be a boy or a girl. When an X-type sperm fertilizes the egg, the baby will be a girl, and when a Y-type sperm enters the egg, it will be a boy. Although this fact is known, there is no way the male or female can influence a specific type of sperm to fertilize the egg.

Multiple Births

Identical twins result when the fertilized egg divides. Since the egg can be fertilized by only one sperm, it means that when division of the egg occurs the chromosomes also divide equally. This equality gives to each divided cell the same formula and same number of chromosomes, thus resulting in the babies being born as nearly alike as it is possible to be. Fraternal twins occur when two eggs are in the Fallopian tube at the same time and are fertilized by two different sperms. They may be fertilized by two X sperms, two Y sperms, or an X and a Y sperm. The possible birth combination in this case is two girl babies, two boy babies, or a girl baby and a boy baby. In any instance, they will not be identical, but will be as much unlike as if they were born years apart.

Dominancy

No one sex is dominant over the other in transmitting characteristics to the offspring.

Concerning the Fetus

The fetus does not breathe inside the mother in the same way as we think of breathing. It must have oxygen, but this is received from the blood of the mother. An unborn baby neither eats nor gets rid of its own waste. Food for the unborn baby is supplied from the mother's own blood stream.

The mother has the responsibility of eating correct foods and keeping in good general health, but in no other way does she influence the developing child. The impression that a woman can mark her child during pregnancy is completely false. The physical and mental characteristics of a baby are mostly the result of the chromosomes and genes.

Artificial Insemination

This method of fertilization should be understood because of its accepted practice in the animal kingdom. Some farmers choose not to keep a bull. Instead, they prefer to use the semen of a bull owned by some other farmer or by a breeders' association. This farmer or association representative is trained and experienced in gathering and storing semen for use in artificial insemination. When the farmer knows one of his cows is in heat, he understands that nature has prepared that cow to be ready to conceive if sperms are made available to fertilize the egg that has ovulated and is in her Fallopian tube. The inseminator puts the especially preserved semen into the cow's vagina near the cervix. When the sperms become motile, they travel to the ovum in the Fallopian tube to fertilize the egg. If a sperm meets an egg, it will fertilize the egg whether it has been released by the artificial insemination method or the natural method. Farmers like the artificial method. The semen used in artificial insemination is from a registered bull, thus helping the farmer to improve the quality of his cows. In human beings, fertilization by artificial insemination can be done in much the same manner. Semen is used from a man known as the donor. He is chosen by the doctor and is unknown to either the husband or the wife. This method of reproduction is used only in instances where the husband is sterile, and he and his wife feel a child born to them in this manner is preferable to an adopted child. However, the social, legal, and religious implications of the artificial insemination method of fertilization are many. Some states regard the child born in this manner as being illegitimate. From a religious point of view this method of having a family raises many questions. It is still recommended that a childless couple go to a recognized agency and adopt a child they both want and in whose love and care they can equally share.

Reasons for Childless Marriages

Very few married people do not want children. However, one of every ten married couples do not have children even though they want them. In these instances the difficulty may lie in either the husband or the wife. The couple probably have no way of knowing the reason for their childlessness. Here again their trusted family doctor should be consulted for causes and possible remedies. A general understanding of sterility and infertility is another phase of sex education. The following definitions of sterility and infertility may be helpful in aiding to understand them: When the inability to have children is a permanent condition, the man or woman is said to be sterile. If the condition can be treated and corrected, it is spoken of as "infertility." This condition may result from any one of several causes. Serious infections due to venereal diseases can block the passage of sperms from the testes, and eggs from the ovaries. When this type of infection is not properly treated, the result will be sterility. Injury to the testes or ovaries may prohibit the proper development of sperms or ova. Exposure of the testes or ovaries to prolonged and excessive radiation destroys their reproductive ability. Illness may cause temporary infertility. This is especially true of the male if the illness involves a high fever. Weeks may be required to bring sperm production back to normal. In the woman the uterus may be tilted in such a position that sperms cannot enter the uterus, thus causing infertility. Obstructions may occur at the cervix, making conception impossible. Whatever the cause of infertility, there is hope through prayer and the knowledge of the medical profession for those who are so affected.

Menopause

Menopause is that period in the life of a woman which marks the end of her ability to have children. It is more commonly known as "the change of life." Many of the changes which occur in menopause are chemical in origin, but they result in marked physical changes. These changes result from the diminished activity of the ovaries in the production of hormones. When the hormone secretion is lessened or withdrawn, the result is a change in secondary sex characteristics, and eventually the production of ova is stopped. The hormones of the pituitary gland are also responsible for body changes in menopause. Menopause may begin when a woman reaches the middle thirties, or it may not start until she reaches her middle fifties, but the average age is forty-five. The menopause resembles puberty in reverse. In some individuals the physical symptoms of menopause are rather trying and uncomfortable. If this be the case, a competent doctor can keep the physical and mental discomforts down to a minimum.

Growing into Maturity

As a Girl

If you are a girl and old enough to be in junior high school, you may have noticed that boys seem to you to be immature and at times childish in the way they talk and behave. Your observation is partially correct, for girls do mature sooner than boys, both physically and socially. Teen-age girls enter into a period of development known as adolescence. In this period the body undergoes growth and development at a very accelerated rate. Because of this rapidity of growth, muscular co-ordination is at times difficult, and awkwardness in activities such as dancing and athletics results. For no apparent reason, fatigue may also be experienced during adolescence. One major body change in this period is the rapid development of the reproductive organs. In addition, the general body structure takes on the appearance of maturity: the breasts develop and fill out; the pelvis increases in width; hair appears under the arms and in the pubic region; the voice becomes mature and richer in tone. This is an age when the whole world seems to be awakening to the excitement of the feel of maturity. New feelings, interests, and desires make life interesting and exciting.

This physical maturing brings with it an entirely new physical experience called menstruation. When menstruation begins, it is a sure sign that womanhood is "just around the corner." The age at which menstruation begins cannot be definitely determined. It may vary between the ages of nine and sixteen. The majority of girls begin to menstruate at the age of thirteen. Menstruation is not something to fear, or about which to be alarmed or disgusted. It is nature's way of letting you know that you will soon be a woman, capable of taking your place in the world as a wife and mother. Understanding menstruation brings an appreciation of the wonderful way nature has endowed women to be mothers.

Menstruation occurs in cycles. Every twenty-eight days an ovum matures in the ovary and is released through the wall of the ovary. This release is called ovulation. The ovaries, like so many other glands of the body, produce hormones. Estrogen, which is a hormone produced by the ovaries, is carried by the blood to the uterus, where it stimulates the wall of the uterus, causing it to thicken. This thickening of the wall is in preparation for pregnancy if fertilization should occur. Progesterone, which is the other hormone produced by the ovaries, is secreted at the time of ovulation, and if fertilization of the ovum occurs, it maintains pregnancy. If, however, the ovum is not fertilized, this build-up of the lining of the uterus cannot serve its purpose. In this case, nature then causes the uterus to shed its lining, which is voided as a mixture of blood and cellular debris. This flow is called menstruation. The normal menstrual flow lasts from three to five days.

As stated before, the normal menstrual cycle occurs every twenty-eight days, but illness, nervous tensions, etc., may cause the cycle to be longer or shorter. If this deviation or irregularity occurs frequently in a teen-age girl, it is advisable that she consult her doctor. Menstruation is not a period during which a woman should consider herself sick and incapacitated. However, it is not advisable to engage in strenuous work, athletics, etc., at this time. With rest and care the normal routine of living is feasible and desirable.

As a Boy

Boys, like girls, also experience physical changes during adolescence. At puberty the penis and testes become larger; the beard begins to appear; the voice deepens; and the general body structure takes on the appearance of a man. Physical strength is developing; but during this transition period poor muscular co-ordination results in awkwardness. This muscular uncertainty is usually prevalent in the eighth grade and freshman year of high school. By the junior year in high school, physical maturity is well established and active sports usually become the center of interest.

Sexual maturity brings with it a new experience in the form of nocturnal emissions. This is a release of semen during sleep. Another term more commonly used than nocturnal emissions is "wet dream." Nocturnal emissions are nothing about which to be alarmed, for it is a perfectly natural occurrence. It is nature's way of releasing sperms which have been stored in the reproductive system.

Another type of sex experience especially related to the teen-age level is that of masturbation. Masturbation is the handling of the sex organs until there is a sexual climax. Masturbation is commonly practiced, but this does not make it right or the desirable thing to do. In fact, there is much to be said against it. In fairness to those who have heard weird tales concerning masturbation, it should be stated that it does not have the harmful effects some people believe it to have. It will not cause insanity, make the person sterile, or cause one's children to be born deformed. Masturbation does have emotional and social implications serious enough to discourage its practice. Some boys and girls use it as an escape mechanism for their social shortcomings. Guilt and shame may accompany its practice, thus further developing personality conflicts. The best solution is for boys and girls to keep busy, have friends and associates, and be interested in things other than themselves. Teen-agers will find that being active in athletics, dramatics, music, church, a hobby, etc., is a useful and interesting way to spend their time. There is nothing abnormal about sex instincts and desires; in fact, it would be abnormal not to have them. However, sex is an instinct that needs to be channeled and controlled, and keeping busy with worthwhile things will be of great help in this respect. To become well-adjusted men and women, young people must learn to form patterns of sex control and behavior.

Dating

"It's a date." No other topic is so popular and thrilling to talk about. The chances are that if a group of teen-age girls are talking, it will be about boys. In like manner, boys sooner or later come around to the discussion of girls. It soon becomes apparent in these discussions that not everyone has the same idea as to what a date is, and what it should mean. To the boy or girl in the eighth grade it means one thing, to the couple going steady it means something else, and to the engaged couple its meaning and purpose are still different.

Have you ever stopped to ask yourself, What is a date? If you are a girl you might say, "A date is when a boy comes to my house to pick me up and we go somewhere and have a good time." This is true, but it is also a date if you and your boy friend stay home with Mother and Dad to watch television or play cards. Some young girls feel that if by chance they meet a boy at the soda fountain and have a coke together, that too is a date; but, strictly speaking, it is not. To be sure, it has many of the characteristics of a date, but it fails to meet the requirement of pre-arrangement. When a date is made, there is a pre-arranged agreement as to the time, place, and activity.

Age for Dating

The age at which to begin dating depends upon many factors. The attitude of your parents concerning dating is one influential factor; another is the speed with which you mature physically and mentally. If you have an older brother or sister who has dated, they may have broken the ice, so to speak, in your family. Girls, as a rule, become interested in dating at an earlier age than boys. Because girls mature physically sooner than boys, it is only natural that they also become interested in dating at an earlier age. This early interest in boys is not without some danger. A girl of thirteen or fourteen may wish to date boys of seventeen or eighteen years of age. A boy this age has had dating experience, and if the boy is the type who is interested in petting and going to undesirable places, the inexperienced girl may be persuaded to do things she would not do if she were older. Age is not always the determining factor as to when dating should begin. Many girls and boys begin to date relatively young; but to do so they should have good training in boy-girl relationships in their home, school, and church. Knowing how to date should be a requisite for being permitted to begin to date.

Dating Experience

Early dating experience is best gained in group activities. For example, your eighth grade or junior-high class may be going on a wiener roast; your Sunday school may be having its yearly picnic, or the neighborhood gang may have decided to go ice skating. In all these activities, most of which are supervised, you get to know the opposite sex through the experience of games, talking together, eating together, and just being around together. It is important for you to learn how each sex acts and thinks. It will not take long for you to discover the difference in people's behavior. Some people are courteous, fair in play, and discreet in conversation, while others are of the opposite behavior. You soon learn what kind of person you will want to date, and you will also experience first-hand the things young people say and do that are embarrassing and not in good taste.

Double Dating

After having the group experience, double dating is the next logical sequence for gaining dating skills. Like group activities, it affords company in sharing and doing, yet it has more intimacy than the group. In fact, it has many of the characteristics of single dating. Double dating is dating on a mature level. It is approved by most parents; and when parents approve, dating is more fun.

Single Dates

Single dates are the ultimate objective in dating. Single dating comes into common practice at about the senior year of high school. This is especially true for boys.

When you begin to have single dates, an entirely new world of experiences and opportunities opens to you. In the terms of aviation, you are now "soloing." Now all the learning and experiences of the past can be put into practice. If your dates are fun and go smoothly, if you have acquired the respect and admiration of the opposite sex, and if your parents approve of your choice of friends, your struggle for independence and success in dating is well on its way.

Dating Skills

Dating experience is a part of the process of growing up. No other activity on the teen-age level gives you the opportunity to learn to know the opposite sex as do the experiences of dating. Dating is a skill that must be learned. You can learn much from couples who are well-mannered, courteous, and considerate of each other, as contrasted to those who are noisy, crude in speech, and lack the fundamentals of acceptable practice. Some teen-age boys may assume it is unimportant to do such things as open the car door for their date, seat her at the table, call for her properly at her home, and meet her parents with ease and friendliness. A girl is anxious for her friends to think well of the boy she dates. She is proud if he uses correct English, has a good vocabulary, dresses neatly, is mature in judgment, and on all occasions gives evidence of culture. Be it boy or girl, lacking these fundamentals constitutes a handicap for successful dating.

When to Ask for a Date

The kind of date determines, to some extent, how far in advance the girl should be asked. Naturally, how well these two people know each other, and the popularity of the girl, are other things to consider. A popular girl might be dated for some weeks in advance. She might be very eager to date the boy, but if he asks for a date only a few days or a week in advance, she may have the date filled. If the date is with a new girl, it is courteous to ask for the date well in advance. Dates involving formal parties need much preparation; therefore a girl is entitled to ample time. Going on a hayride or on a skating party requires planning, but not to the extent of dates involving more exacting social dress.

What to Do on a Date

Does it make any difference what is done on a date? Is it not enough that two people are just together? The answers to these questions are the answers to why dates fail. What is done on a date is very important to the success of the date. What you can do and want to do on a date is influenced by such factors as weather, time of the year, money, interests, availability of a car, attitude of your parents, age, whether your date is a casual one, or whether you are going steady, or are engaged. The things that are possible to do on a date are limited only by the ingenuity and resourcefulness of the couple.

Where to go and what to do are problems faced by all dating couples. School functions afford many opportunities and, as a rule, find favor with parents. Athletic events are always a possibility, and the setting is ideal for a good time. School loyalty and being with friends of mutual interest makes the date go well. Other school possibilities are talent shows, proms, plays, musicals, and club picnics. Obviously, not all dates should be school-centered. A sampling of other dating possibilities are: movies, television, musical concerts, horseback riding, bowling, hayrides, ice and roller skating, amusement parks, cards, social games, etc. All too often the possibility of bringing a date to church is overlooked. Going to church together is stimulating. In addition to providing worship services, most churches have facilities and organizations which appeal to young people.

It is all too frequently assumed that it is necessary to go places and spend money in order to have a successful date. Wonderful times can be had at church-sponsored activities, with little or no cost. A real bargain is the home date, where father and mother provide food and facilities. Home dates can be real fun. Watching television, playing games with the family, baking a batch of cookies, making candy, listening to records, singing, playing the piano, popping corn, or just talking is fun — if it is not idle gossip.

Responsibility for Planning a Date

Boys and girls are often confused as to who is responsible for determining what to do on a date. As a rule, the boy should suggest the activity if it is his first date with the girl. He has assumed the leadership in asking for the date, and he should suggest what he would like to do. If the girl does not warmly approve his suggestion, the boy should have other possibilities in mind. These alternatives give the girl and her parents a little more information concerning the feasibility of the date. If the couple know each other well and have been dating each other, mutual planning is the most satisfactory.

Conversation

Do you experience difficulty in keeping conversation going, especially if your date is a person you have never dated before? Many people have this difficulty, but fortunately it is easily solved. A logical place to begin in becoming acquainted is to find out what you have in common. In all probability you will find that you share many interests or experiences. If you attend the same school, it is possible that you took the same course or had the same teachers at some time. Perhaps the school talent show is being organized and both of you are working on an act. The coming football game with a city rival has the whole school talking, and you find you are no exception. You further discover that both of you like church and Sunday school, and that opens up new opportunities for discussion and mutual understanding. Some common mistakes must be avoided if the date is to go smoothly. If you are a boy, it is inexcusable to overemphasize your own exploits and interests. Your girl friend may not be as interested as you think in the number of touchdowns you scored in the last game, or the number of times you made the headlines. It is equally bad to talk about nothing but your hot-rod automobile — most girls are not interested in dual carburetors, changed gear ratio, or custom body design. If you are a girl, you, too, can be out of order by making yourself the center of interest, or telling your boy friend how well your last date danced. Your club sisters may be interesting to you, but your date may rather talk about things and people you both know.

Drinking

Drinking is a question that must be considered in a discussion of dating. Drinking, in the eyes of the law, is not illegal if the person is of age. The law does impose restrictions on minors. The Bible has not condemned the moderate use of alcohol as being immoral or wrong, if done discreetly and in a manner not offensive to others. However, drinking can lead to immorality, and it can be a source of danger when driving a car. So-called "social drinking" is common in almost all groups of young people, yet this does not necessarily make it acceptable or exemplary. If you, a boy or girl, have convictions against drinking of any kind, you need not apologize for taking a forthright stand. It is your duty to protest against the silly remarks, boisterous behavior, and show-off attitudes of one under the influence of alcohol; but diplomacy must be used with those who are in their legal rights and are conducting themselves in an acceptable manner. To be realistic, little can be said in favor of using alcoholic beverages. Drinking is not a symbol of manliness, nor does it show the ability to do something unusual and different. Any high school student learns from a health text that alcohol affects judgments, decreases clarity of vision, and slows muscular co-ordination. Drinking also affects the ability to distinguish right from wrong in matters pertaining to fairness, social behavior, and sex behavior. There have been many regrets resulting from a temporary letdown in judgment and standards while one was under the influence of alcohol.

Smoking

To smoke or not to smoke, that is the question. Smoking does not have the physical, mental, and social hazards of drinking, yet it must be considered a social concern for teen-age people. There are numerous reasons why people smoke. Some teen-age people feel that smoking is a sign of having grown up, and they are trying to prove to themselves that they are old

43

enough "to take it," so to speak. Others claim it is relaxing to their nerves, while still others feel they must smoke to be sociable. The health factor of smoking must be considered. Some authorities feel that smoking does little harm, while others are convinced that it is dangerous. Indications are that there is a correlation between lung cancer and smoking. Athletic coaches know from experience that boys who are heavy smokers are not in top physical condition. Regardless of the arguments for and against smoking, what should be the attitude concerning smoking on a date?

Some people take offense at smoking. A boy on a date with a girl who prefers that he do not smoke should do her the courtesy not to smoke in her presence. Not all boys smoke, and some prefer that their girl friends do not smoke. Here, too, the girl should not give offense to her date by smoking. The situation frequently arises when those who do not smoke are offered a cigarette. What should you do? Refusing a cigarette is not difficult. A polite and courteous "No, thank you, I do not smoke," is all that is needed. You will not be considered odd if you refuse a cigarette. On the contrary, you will be admired by some people for upholding your convictions. Advertisements usually picture smoking as the ultimate in satisfaction and pleasure, but to those who are not interested in smoking, cigarette advertising is not very convincing. Smoking is not a moral issue, but there is little proof of its value.

Some Dates Fail

In spite of all that can be done, occasionally a dating situation arises which is unpleasant. When this occurs, it is a test of your ability to cope with a trying situation. It also is an excellent opportunity to test your poise, tact, or control of temper. Life will present many challenges of personality conflicts and embarrassing situations. Your ability to meet these conflicts and situations will, in a way, determine how well you succeed in getting along with people.

Concluding a Date

The time to be in from a date may be a source of worry and irritation between parents and children. Much depends upon the rules of parents, age of the boy or girl, and the kind of date. If the date happens to be the senior ball held after graduation exercises from high school, it is conceivable that the date could last until morning and still have the parents' consent. Special entertainment and the traditional breakfast make it a lengthy occasion, and both parents and school officials know it is well supervised and carried on in the best social tradition. If the date is just going to a neighborhood movie, the hour to be back home is quite another matter. The age of the dating couple needs to be considered in determining how late a date should last. Freshman boys and girls should not expect, nor be permitted, to have dates as late as seniors. Maturity brings with it privileges and responsibilities not possible at a younger age. If your parents know and trust the boy or girl you are dating, they will be more understanding. A girl's parents might be willing to permit a date to be later if the boy is dependable and mature in judgment. Occasionally an unforeseen situation arises on a date and makes it impossible to get home at the agreed time. In this case, your parents will welcome a call to let them know the cause of delay and that all is well and they need not be alarmed.

Some young people resent the interest their parents have in them, and interpret their parents' concern as mistrusting them and prying into their private affairs. In some instances this might be true; however, most parents are not unduly inquisitive but are concerned only about the welfare of their children.

The time a date should end is the joint responsibility of both the boy and the girl. If the parents have given rules concerning time, they too should be honored. When both dating parties and parents are agreed, there is little room for embarrassment and misunderstanding. You as a boy must use good judgment concerning your date's wishes. She may wish to end the date, but hesitates to do so because of offending you. If you keep a girl on a date until she is obliged to make you leave, you have the wrong concept of dating behavior.

Foot in the Door

The hour is late. Should you, the boy, be invited into the house or expect to be invited in? Here again circumstances affect the situation. If your friend's parents are up, and the following day is not a school day, she may wish to invite you in to share with her parents the good time you both have had. You should realize the situation and not expect to come in if it will be embarrassing to the girl or her parents.

Kissing

No means of expressing affection has been publicized and talked about more than kissing. To kiss or not to kiss, that is the dilemma. Does a boy take it for granted that the girl will kiss? Does a girl take it for granted that the boy will try to kiss? If he does try, and she refuses, what are the chances for another date? Would she, in fact, want another date with him?

46

These questions seem to be involved on the first date a couple have with each other. How do girls feel about the problem? Girls seem to feel that if the date was a success and they liked the boy, a good-night kiss is in order. However, they feel strongly about being kissed against their wishes. A boy should never consider a kiss as a reward for a few dollars spent on a date. Kissing is a means of showing affection, and the girl may not be ready to show this affection. If she refuses to kiss, this does not necessarily mean that she does not like the boy or will refuse him another date. Expressing one's appreciation for a good time can be done without a kiss. In fact, an insincere kiss, or a kiss which gives the impression of passion rather than affection, will do much to ruin what has been a successful evening. A boy who refuses to date a girl for the second time because she did not kiss him needs to re-evaluate his social and moral standards.

How Many Dates

How often should you have a date? This is a perplexing problem for high school people and parents as well. Is one date a week sufficient? Are two or more dates too many? No definite answer can be made, as each situation must be judged separately. One thing is sure, if dates interfere with good schoolwork they should be curtailed. Doing your best in school is your major responsibility, and anything that interferes with it is out of order. Dating should fit into the school schedule. When dating is done during the week, the hours should be such that they do not seriously interfere with schoolwork. When a boy and girl are together too much, they create a situation in which they become so involved that marriage appears to be their only solution.

Never a Date

There are some high school students who have never had a date. This is not recommended, for learning to be natural and at ease with members of the opposite sex is best acquired by associating with them. If marriage is to become a reality someday, it will need to have its beginning in dating. If you are one who has never dated, the fault might be yours; if so, correct it. If the fault lies with your parents, be patient.

Going Steady

"I am going steady." What a familiar expression this is among junior and senior high-school boys and girls! Going steady implies that by mutual consent neither of the couple will have dates with anyone else. Is going steady the desirable thing to do? What are the advantages and disadvantages of going steady? One advantage which is frequently mentioned in favor of going steady is that a date is always assured. There will be no jangled nerves over the weekend because of waiting for the telephone to ring with a date in the offing. A second reason for going steady is that the date will be with someone you know, and you will be reasonably sure of having a good time. The third reason given for steady dating is that going steady saves time and money. Money is an important item when one is dating. At best, most boys in high school have only a part-time job. When two people go steady, they feel they know each other well and can speak freely of their financial status. The girl may offer to share expenses, or possibly her parents have been persuaded to have plenty of food on hand for the stay-at-home date. Some young people also feel that going steady develops a feeling of pair unity — a type of possessiveness not possible in casual dating.

It would seem that going steady has all favorable points and nothing detrimental. This, most certainly, is not true. Unless the "steady" is an unusual person, weeks and months together often bring boredom and irritations which dull the glamour of the person who was "perfect" just a few months ago. "What a wonderful thing it would be if I could date Judy, the new cheer leader, instead of having to date only Sue." "Tom, the president of the student council, seems interested in me, but I cannot accept a date so long as I am going steady with Ralph" — and so it goes. Going steady in the freshman year is especially bad because it deprives one of having the opportunity of learning the personalities and ways of many different boys and girls.

It is easy to become involved into going steady and, more or less, taking things for granted. This is especially true when a girl dates an older boy, because he has been exploring the field for some time and now wants the security of a steady girl. Teen-age years with their carefree life, abounding health, and worlds of new experiences should not be sacrificed in assuming an adult role for which the body is not mature and the mind not ready. When, in the future, marriage becomes a reality, it is good to be able to say, "I had my choice, but now I have met and selected the right one."

Breaking Up

A problem faced by those who go steady and then want to break up is the difficulty of doing so without hurting each other's feelings. They still want to be friends, but not steady "dates." Breaking up can be done by a heart-to-heart talk, both admitting that they have grown tired of each other, and that meeting new friends would be best for both. Occasionally, one of the couple does not want to break up. This person should realize that when affection and love are a one-way situation, the relationship cannot endure very long. Breaking up need not be a catastrophe. Young hearts mend rapidly, and when new and interesting things have been discovered, the former romance may even seem a bit silly. It may take time to get back into "circulation," but this can be accomplished by letting your friends know you are no longer going steady, and also by associating with groups other than the "going-steady crowd." Feeling sorry for yourself is not a solution. There are many ways of overcoming this disappointment. Take a vacation; rediscover the fun of reading; become active in church and other organizations to change the emphasis from self-pity to doing things with and for others. To speed and ease this transition process, it is best to destroy old love letters, remove pictures and gifts, or anything that brings back memories. It is surprising how quickly time erases old feelings and memories, and substitutes new and better ones. Life is a continual change; this lesson must be learned early in life for ready adjustment.

Petting

The teen-age is a time when the sex drive is strong and difficult to control. Petting is a type of sex behavior which becomes so powerful and compelling that everything else which can be done on a date seems trivial and uninteresting. People who love each other have every right to show affection. To love is fun, and the showing of affection is part of it. Loving each other is as old as man. But some young people think they have discovered something new — something that father and mother have never experienced and are too old to understand. Showing of affection can take many different forms, some of which are acceptable and others not. The type of love and affection mother and father have and experience is different and more mature than the romantic-type love of dating days.

Every generation expresses its love-making in different terms. Your parents, or other adults of comparable age, called their love-making "necking." To you, the teen-ager, terms like "pitching" and "making-out" are more up to date. These newer terms may sound very unacceptable to your parents, but in reality, they mean nothing different than "necking." All of these expressions refer to the usual holding of hands, hugging and kissing, or, in other words, nothing extreme. Petting, however, is unacceptable because its purpose is to rouse sex. Petting refers to handling or caressing parts of the body for the purpose of sex stimulation, and if it is practiced with consistency it eventually leads to sex relations. The psychological effects of petting may be very disturbing.

Many teen-agers want to know what is so wrong with petting or even having sex relations before marriage, because they know acquaintances who seem to be enjoying these experiences. The answer is not simple, for it not only involves spiritual principles and ideals, but also has physical and mental implications. The sex instinct should not be considered as something "dirty" or wrong. In fact, it is God's creation and He has made it an integral part of the human process of reproduction. When sex is correctly shared by husband and wife, it brings them an expression of love that can be acquired in no other way. If this be true of man and wife, why then is this experience not approved for the unmarried? An indisputable reason is plainly given in the Bible, where we read in Exodus 20:14, "Thou shalt not commit adultery." Sex relations outside the married estate are adultery. To you who live by the teachings of Christ this should be sufficient reason. Many may, however, take religious principles lightly and do not feel bound by Bible teachings. But there are other strong reasons and arguments against petting and against sex relations before marriage.

Petting rouses the nervous system to a high state of tension. When it is not eased or relieved, it leaves the individual nervous, frustrated, unsatisfied, and with a sense of guilt. The sex instinct is very strong and can be roused to a point where judgment and resistance and best intentions are no longer safeguards. Intelligence and education mean little when petting progresses to a point where sex emotions become the ruling factor. There is danger, however, in assuming that any show of affection is wrong. When this concept is pursued, frigidity may take the place of normal sex adjustment. A frigid person is a poor marital risk. To the sexually maladjusted person, sex relations have no meaning and enjoyment but rather shame and disgust. God created man with a sex instinct and with a purpose for its use, but he also created man with a conscience and a mind so as to use sex in accordance with His will. It is unfortunate but true that some people disregard or ignore God's will and assume they are old enough, wise enough, and independent enough to live as they choose. Even to these people who feel they are rulers of their own destiny, sex relations before marriage are fraught with many dangers and disappointments.

The fear of being caught doing what society and religion condemn as wrong brings with it many apprehensions. Carrying on sex relations in haste and with guilt complexes most assuredly is not building up the kind of sex patterns and appreciations found in marriage. Sex, for its fullest meaning, requires love, cooperation, and an environment not possible under conditions outside of marriage. The fact is that sex experiences in "lovers' lane" may well be more disgusting than pleasurable. What was expected to be the ultimate of all experiences turns out to be animalistic in behavior and painful to endure. The woman may well assume that if sex in marriage is like this, she will want no part of it.

Another reason for continence is the risk of pregnancy. Some young people, especially boys, think they have the answer in the use of contraceptives. The testimony of many pregnant girls should be sufficient evidence to prove that boys can be wrong. Some engaged couples feel that sex relations before marriage are justified because it helps them to determine whether they are suited for each other. This concept is wrong, for sex cannot be correctly experienced under forbidden circumstances. The man or woman demanding sex relations before marriage has selfishness, not love, as a motivating factor. Love does not demand the sacrifice of principles that are right. When sex is practiced before marriage, passion, not love, is the dominant motivating force. When just being together, sharing each other's interests in sports, music, books, drama, and the other fine things of life, run a poor second to the thrill of petting and sex experimentation before marriage, then a possible marriage is doomed to failure.

Sex life of human beings is on an entirely different plateau from that of animals. It has dignity and character motivated by a love and understanding not possible for animals. This being true, human beings use sex not only for propagation but also as an expression of love and devotion between husband and wife. In the animal kingdom, cats, dogs, cattle, horses, etc., will have sex relations only when the female is in heat. Being in heat means that the ovaries of the animal have ovulated a mature ovum which is ready to be fertilized. This is the only time the female is interested in the male. Sex relations in animals have only one purpose: propagation. Love does not enter into the sex life of animals. Human beings, on the other hand, have the privilege of engaging in sex at their discretion and are not dependent upon a definite cycle of ovulation. Copulation, to be sure, is primarily for the purpose of reproduction, but in addition it becomes a mutual expression of love and all the finer things in life for man and wife. To the unmarried, whether of teen-age or older, engaging in sex before marriage is not in accord with social approval or God's will, and it certainly is not the expression of true love before marriage.

Dr. Thurman Rice,[1] who was an outstanding authority on sex education and also a pioneer in the state of Indiana in promoting sex education in high schools, colleges, and churches, once told the following story: On one occasion he was asked to address a college assembly on sex education. After his remarks, an engaged couple came to him and said they were going

---

[1] Formerly professor at Indiana University School of Medicine and head of Indiana State Board of Health.

to be married in three months, but the desire to have sex relations before this time was so strong that they felt they could not wait. Dr. Rice congratulated them on their engagement and love for each other. He then asked whether they had all their wedding plans completed, and whether they were going to have a reception after the wedding. Enthusiastically they answered in the affirmative and told him about the special cake and ice cream they were going to have for the occasion. Dr. Rice then made this suggestion to them: "Do not wait until the reception to cut the cake, but invite your friends and relatives in during the coming week and have a pre-wedding celebration." The couple expressed surprise at such an absurd suggestion. Dr. Rice said no more and left. Three months later he received a post card from this same couple, who were now on their honeymoon. It read, "Thank you, Dr. Rice! We saw the point; we did not cut our wedding cake in advance."

Life consists of regulations, decisions, restrictions, and controls. There are many things to which we must conform if we want to maintain good spiritual, mental, and physical health. Eating, drinking, playing, etc., must all be in moderation. The body with its various functions is a marvelous machine, but it breaks down under abuse. We cannot do with it as we wish, and what is equally important, we would not be happy if we could. Imagine, if you can, what our society would be like and what our family and friends would be like if everyone had complete freedom to do with sex as he pleased. Love would give way to lust, and the law of the jungle would prevail. Only when sex is used as God intended it to be used can it have its fullest meaning. Thousands of young people will testify that well-planned dates, mutual respect, devotion to parents, and love for God in no way deterred them from having the enjoyment of youth they have every right to experience. To those who have kept this faith, sex in marriage will be a richer experience.

What If the Sex Line Has Been Crossed?

What is the situation of young people who have already used sex as their idea of fun and entertainment before marriage? What is the hope of those who want to mend their ways? Certainly they cannot be condemned to permanent disgrace and offered no hope for a successful marriage. The answer lies in faith and in the belief that God forgives all sins for Jesus' sake to those who truly repent. It is easy to condemn those who have sinned, and to take a "more righteous than thou" attitude. In John 8:1-11 the Bible relates the story of the adulterous woman, and in the seventh verse Jesus says: "He that is without sin among you, let him first cast a stone at her." The hope for the future is never closed to those who sincerely want to make amends. It cannot, however, be too strongly emphasized that the couple entering marriage with no past to hide from each other is starting life together in a way for which there is no substitute.

Prostitution

If all people lived in accordance with the moral code, diseases such as syphilis and gonorrhea would have little chance of spreading. In fact, they would become as extinct as the once dreaded smallpox. Venereal diseases have been a scourge to man for centuries. A link in this unbroken chain has been that of prostitution. A prostitute is a woman who for a certain sum of money offers her body to men for sexual gratification. In other words, sex is her profession. Prostitution to the unthinking girl may appear to be an easy way of making a living. To a teen-age boy or a man a prostitute may appear to be the answer to a strong, unsatisfied sex urge. Prostitution, however, not only wrecks the human body but it also distorts the entire concept of the purpose of sex. Prostitutes are, in reality, slaves to men. It is true, some few women of this type may seem to be popular, have plenty of money, and appear to lead a life of ease and luxury. However, as in all cases where sin is involved, the wages of sin will eventually be unhappiness and suffering. The once glamorous prostitute soon finds her attractive body losing its appeal, and she has learned with regret that the animal instinct of man is not love. The inevitable happens. Her loss of beauty and appeal means loss of money and moving to less and less desirable locations. She can now only attract the type of man who has himself sunk to her status or below. However, not all blame for following a life of prostitution should be laid to the woman. A teen-age boy or a man who starts a girl on the road to sex relations before marriage may be the more guilty one. The girl may be led to believe that popularity and desirability go hand in hand with sex. If, however, marriage for her does not follow these escapades, life to her suddenly becomes useless and hopeless. She becomes bitter and resentful, and prostitution seems the only way out. One unfortunate by-product of prostitution and even promiscuity is that of contracting venereal diseases: syphilis or gonorrhea. These diseases are known as venereal diseases because they are transmitted by sexual relations or infection.

Syphilis

Syphilis is a disease which has left its trail of suffering and death through the ages. However, with the progress of medical science in this field the suffering and the death rate can be greatly reduced. Unfortunately, now, as in the past, many of those who contract syphilis hesitate to go to competent medical authority for help. Syphilis is no respecter of persons, be they rich, poor, young, or old. In the United States 76 out of every 100,000 people have syphilis, but in large cities perhaps twice that number. Those in their late teens and early twenties account for the highest percentage. This is a severe indictment of the morals of youth who have reached an age when life offers abundant health and the brightest future.

It is essential to know the cause and symptoms of syphilis in order to understand it thoroughly. Syphilis is caused by a corkscrewlike organism called a spirochete. This germ is contracted from the infected person during sex relations. The symptoms of syphilis are well known. A few days after sexual contact with one who has syphilis, a sore, called a chancre, appears on the penis of the male or labia of the female. But many people who become infected do not seek medical care; instead, they try some home or patent-medicine remedy. Regardless of what is done or not done, the chancre will heal and disappear. But in those who do not get medical care, the syphilis germ remains active in the body. After the disappearance of the chancre the disease goes into the second stage with such symptoms as skin rash, headaches, sore throat, and white patches on the membranes of the mouth. The third and last stage is a deceptive one in which the spirochetes lie dormant for many years. In this last stage syphilis is often referred to as the "great masquerader," because in this stage it can affect the nervous system and result in paralysis or insanity. Blindness may also result, and many a heart attack has been the result of a long-time syphilitic infection. A pregnant woman infected with syphilis may give birth to a deformed and retarded child, and in some instances the baby is born dead. For such a woman, however, there is hope if she will go to a medical doctor before the fifth month of pregnancy. By submitting to proper treatment she will protect her baby from the ill effects of syphilis. Medical science is doing wonders for the cure of syphilis, but it must be emphasized again and again that there is no substitute for good morality. State governments recognize the tragedy of syphilis, and many require a blood test before a marriage license can be obtained. This is a good law and it helps discover some syphilitic cases, but it does not benefit the people who do not get married and are not subject to the blood test.

Gonorrhea

Gonorrhea is another venereal disease contracted by sex relations. In the larger metropolitan areas as many as 250 persons per 100,000 contract the disease. This infection is caused by a type of microorganism known as the cocci group — a pus-forming bacillus. The gonococcus bacillus, one of this group, is the organism which causes gonorrhea. Gonorrhea infects the moist mucous membranes of the genital tract. In the female, the urethra becomes infected, causing a burning sensation when urinating. The vagina also is attacked, and eventually it spreads to the uterus and

Fallopian tubes. When the Fallopian tubes become badly infected, their passage is blocked to such an extent that the ovum from the ovary cannot be reached by the sperm, thus causing sterility in the woman. In very severe cases, when the abdominal cavity is infected, peritonitis results. As in the female, gonorrhea may also involve the urethra in the male. Infection can close the vasa deferentia, causing the man to be sterile.

A newborn baby's eyes are protected from gonorrhea by placing a few drops of weak silver nitrate into its eyes as soon as it is born. This prevents the blindness which results when the mother is infected with gonorrhea.

Love

The word "love" is a term used by almost everyone, yet no two people interpret it to mean exactly the same thing. What love means to us is influenced by our home background, sex, age, experience, education, and religion. To a freshman girl love means something different than to a senior girl. A mother interprets love differently than does her daughter, and grandmother's version is again different. Love changes in meaning and expression with age and experience. It may be difficult to analyze love and to define it in a sentence, but it is real enough to be studied and discussed.

Love plays a part in our life from the moment of birth until death. The Bible refers to love many, many times, not only with regard to the love of God, but also to the love men should have for God and for one another. If true love, instead of armed might, were the dominating force among people and nations, the whole social order of the world would be changed for the better. The love we wish to discuss here, however, is the type of love we experience as brothers, sisters, husband, wife, and sweetheart.

Everyone loves himself or herself; this love had its origin when we were babies. Babies love their voice, toes, fingers, and almost everything about themselves. In many ways self-love is selfish. The entire interest of a baby is self-centered. When baby is hungry, wet, or uncomfortable in any way, it seeks attention by crying, and it makes little difference to the baby whether the mother is busy or tired. A baby is interested only in itself; it must become more mature ·and experienced to offer love in return for favors and affection shown to it. How then do we develop love as we know it on the adult level?

The first lover for most of us was our mother, whose attention, sacrifices, and affection have made a lasting impression. Much of our concept of love was acquired at an early age, long before we were actually conscious of love and its emotional implications.

Father's love for us also played an important role in our early life. He helped Mother feed us, clothe us, and put us to bed. The way he played with us, brought us surprises, and fixed our toys were also expressions of love which helped influence us. There can be little doubt that our parents influenced our concept of love — each parent in a different way and for different things.

Brothers and sisters also had their influence on our meaning of love. Playing together and even quarreling with each other developed a bond of family unity that can be acquired in no other way. Big brother or little sister might have been a nuisance at times, but through them a type of love and understanding was developed that is carried throughout life.

Growing up, however, was not done entirely within the confines of the family. Playmates in the neighborhood and at school exerted their influence on us, and we began to know and love them in one way or another. Attachments at this age centered very strongly in our friends. Some of our closest friends shared our secrets, and we gave them our undivided loyalty. This behavior was not abnormal but a part of growing up and progressing from one level of maturity to another.

Junior-high age is the age of hero worship, and frequently a teacher is the object of affection. No one seemed quite so nice as the physical education teacher with his or her understanding of your problems. Then, too, this teacher had the physical skill and athletic ability so admired by children of this age. Others who received your admiration (which is a form of love) were famous people or "stars" in the field of television, movies, or sports. These people set the patterns for your thinking and doing; you wanted to follow their occupations, copy their hair styles, sing their records, etc. In your hero worship days your idols could do no wrong — their ways were your ways.

Time moves on and you enter high school. Here a whole new world is opened up with experiences of freedom and maturity which are wonderful. You are on your own, spending your money for lunch as you see fit, buying your own books, and choosing your own friends. The giggly and silly days of the freshman year soon pass to the "know-it-all" stage of the sophomore year with its new thrills and experiences. Boys begin to take some notice of girls, but to the girls of this age, boys are beginning to be "all that matters." The sophomore girl is fast becoming a woman of fine physique and beauty; love, with its awakening, is becoming a compelling force. In the junior and senior year, boy-girl relationships begin to take on added meaning, and love seems something different from what it was before. A particular boy or girl may suddenly become intensely interesting and exciting, and living is romance with a capital R. Love seems serious and uncontrollable, and it occupies most of your thoughts and interests. Love seems to be the most wonderful thing in the world; and then again, its hurts are so cruel that survival seems impossible. What, then, is this thing called love? Does it make sense? To understand and appreciate this impelling emotion a more detailed study is necessary.

The expression "falling in love" is a common one, but it is seldom a true one. In reality, we grow into love. "Falling" implies something sudden, violent, and unexpected; but this is not the way love usually begins. It is possible that interest in another person might be sudden, but when this happens, it resembles infatuation more than love.

Infatuation is largely physical and material. It has as its impelling force such factors as the color and sparkle of the eyes, athletic ability, popularity, a sweet smile; or it might be a new sports convertible which "ignites the spark" of infatuation. There is nothing wrong or bad about infatuation if it is recognized in time as such. It is misleading when it is interpreted as love. Infatuation has marks of identification which are helpful in distinguishing it from real love. It usually lasts but a short time; parents and friends recognize it as a passing fancy rather than love; infatuation is self-centered and relies on social and sexual excitement for its survival. Infatuation is "part of love," but not enough of the "whole of love" to be self-sustaining.

Real love does not come as suddenly as thunder and lightning; it is gradual and has a firm foundation. Love is very complex and does not mean the same thing to all people. Our conception of love, as we have seen, has been influenced by many factors. The way our parents expressed their love to each other, to their children, and to friends gave us our earliest impression of love. The friends with whom we associated as children, our school training, our educational interests, our religious background, the sincerity with which we live our religious convictions, God's love manifested in so many ways — all these are factors which have influenced our love. In fact, there is little of our past and present that is not in some way influential in molding us as a person and determining what we think, say, and do about love. It follows that if a boy has a good mother whom he loves, the qualities of love he will seek in a wife must measure up, in a high degree, to those of his mother. A girl who has lived in a home where a drunken father mistreated the mother will not accept drinking and drunkenness as part of love. We tend to fall in love with people who make us feel comfortable and happy, and who remind us of things and experiences that are pleasing to us.

This question is frequently asked: Is there just one person in the world with whom we can fall in love and be happily married? Certainly every couple who have learned to love each other and married feel that each has found the "one and only." If, however, the two had lived in a different locality and had never met, they would have fallen in love with someone else. We fall in love with someone we meet and with whom we become acquainted intimately enough to discover that he meets the qualifications and ideals we are looking for in a marriage partner. We fall in love only with those we meet and learn to know.

It is not likely that a woman who comes from a wealthy family and who has had the finest education will marry a man who quit school at age sixteen because of failing subjects or disciplinary action. He would not fulfill her concept of what she wants in a husband. This does not imply that people who quit school at an early age may not be good citizens or good husbands and wives. It does imply, however, that people with different concepts and backgrounds are not likely to fall in love. It is no accident that farm boys fall in love with farm girls; they have much in common. They know and appreciate each other's way of life — the work, sacrifices, joys, and disappointments that go with farming. A woman who was born and reared in a large city, and whose only experience of growing things was confined to a flower in an apartment window, and whose only contact with animals was the family cat, is not likely to have in her concept of love a life which means getting up with the sun and doing the chores of a farmer's wife. Falling in love will be more favorable if two people share each other's religious beliefs and have much the same social and economic background.

Love is not something over which we have no control; it must not leave us helpless, irrational, and drifting as a ship without a rudder. Instead, we must understand it, know its purpose, and use it for the achievement of the finer things in life. When love is understood, it is never taken for granted. It must be continually experienced and practiced in order to be kept alive. Love, if left uncultivated, soon finds itself choked out by the weeds of indifference and mistrust. Like life itself, love grows and flourishes with care and use, but dies with neglect.

Tests of Love

How do I know whether I am in love? How can I tell whether he or she loves me? These haunting questions confront young adults sooner or later. The answer is not a simple one; yet certain characteristics of love help to answer these questions. The following twelve items will aid in diagnosing love:

1. It is not likely to be real love if you are in your early teens. Love of the adult variety requires maturity. This maturity does not come until the late teens or early twenties – more likely the latter.

2. Love is concerned with the "We" and not with the "I." Love is not selfish. If you are in love, the person you love is all-important to you. His or her success is placed above your own. The good fortune or abilities of the one you love are never a source of envy but rather one of joy to you.

3. Love brings with it a sense of personal happiness and satisfaction. Happiness, because you and the one you love agree on the things in life which are important to both of you. Satisfaction, because you have found each other, and your energies can now be directed toward "growing" and planning the future together.

4. Love ought to be realistic. No person is perfect or can be made perfect. Every individual has weaknesses and faults; yet these must be within the limits of what is acceptable to you.

5. You will be proud of your lover. You will be

eager to have your friends meet him, and you will want them to know what he stands for — his abilities, hopes, ideals, and ambitions. This also applies to a man's feeling about the woman he loves and intends to marry.

6. Love is real if you have the desire to share with each other the better things in life. If you read a good book, you want to share it with your loved one. A vacation is more fun if you can take it together, and a movie or play becomes alive if you see it in each other's company.

7. Mature love is in agreement concerning morals and religion. It is possible to love each other without professing a religious faith, but a love which shares faith will experience a depth not attainable when the source of love comes only from what the material world has to offer.

8. People in love want each other's companionship, and just being together is satisfying. It is not love if the companionship must be kept alive by the necessity of going places and doing things for excitement. The depth of love is not measured by how much money is spent or the thrills experienced.

9. Lovers do have quarrels. If they never have quarreled, it would indicate that the opinions of one or the other are being suppressed. An occasional quarrel is not to be feared. In fact, it is a necessity to test whether differences can be resolved. It is not the quarrel that is important, but how it is resolved.

10. Love is not indestructible. Love in full bloom will wither and die if the source of its power is cut off by deceit and doubt.

11. Love is of many kinds. The puppy love of the junior-high age is a type of love which is good to have

experienced, but the more mature, conjugal love of husband and wife is necessary in marriage. Conjugal love has a depth and sincerity not found in the romantic love expressed in the movies. Love should be of the type that is felt without saying a word; every little action, every gesture, has a meaning and understanding.

12. Time is the real test of love. If there is any doubt about the love you have for each other, time will be the deciding factor. No two people can be sure of their love until they have given themselves time to experience being together under a variety of situations. Good behavior and guarded actions are possible for a time, but months or even years together bring out situations that cannot be camouflaged.

Thinking It Through

Choosing a Marriage Partner

Time marches on and soon comes the responsibility for a young adult to decide what he or she wants and needs in a husband or wife. Few decisions in life will be of more far-reaching significance. Marriage is for life, and to marry the wrong person creates situations which may be impossible to correct. Selecting a marriage partner should not be left to chance or impulsive decisions. Life's span being lengthened, you can expect to live with your marriage partner forty years and longer. Surely this realization is reason enough to ponder well and long the question of choosing a partner. It is true that most people, when they consider marriage, have some kind of concept of the person they wish to marry. Is this concept realistic and attainable?

Marriage is not a dream world in which a woman can assume that her husband will fulfill her every desire and wish, nor can the man assume the same of his wife. The wife may wish her husband to be a good dancer, athletic, and own the latest sports convertible. There is nothing wrong with having these desires, but they are unimportant as fundamental requisites of a good husband. It is much more important that the husband have a pleasing personality, good health, religion, ambition, and be interested in family life. The husband may consider physical attraction, popularity, or the ability to play bridge well as essential qualities in a wife. However, other qualities such as friendliness, understanding, health, religion, desire for children, etc., are infinitely more important for establishing a good home. It is assumed that every marriage is based on love; but in choosing a marriage partner similarity of background, interests, religion, ideals, and standards of living are other points to consider.

Looking for perfection in a marriage partner is an error that can cause much unhappiness and keep many fine people from getting married. Settling for mediocrity is not desirable, but a woman should realize that her selection of a husband is definitely limited if her standards are such that only a small per cent of men can qualify. It may be practically impossible to find a man who has a college education, good looks, a large bank roll, and who would be willing to do a major share of the housework.

To have no minimum set of standards is equally undesirable. People change little in personality and behavior patterns after reaching maturity, and to assume the marriage ceremony waves a magic wand to erase all that is bad will prove very disappointing.

A man or woman who is not willing to change before marriage will not likely do so after marriage. Love overlooks and tolerates much, but it cannot withstand the corrosive effect of constant strife and major or minor frictions.

Basic Human Needs

What you need in a husband or wife depends in a large measure on your strengths and weaknesses, but you, like all other people, need love, a sense of personal worth, and a feeling of being wanted. Man and wife each need a love which understands and appreciates the other — a love which needs not the constant repetition of "I love you," expressed so glibly under the competition of the dating days. True love between husband and wife is a love that grows in depth and appreciation, and does not diminish under the challenges that every home experiences.

Security

Security is another basic human need, possibly more so for the wife than for the husband. Man, by nature and tradition, is the aggressor and is permitted more liberties in our way of life than is the woman. If a husband doesn't like his job, he is free to find another. Even in moral behavior, society is much more charitable with the sins of the man than of the woman. In no case, however, can marriage be happy without security. The wife who must put up with her husband's gambling, drinking, and indifference toward his family cannot feel secure. On the other hand, if the husband is to be successful, he must find help, happiness, and understanding at home.

A Sense of Personal Worth

Whether married or single, we need to feel a sense of personal worth. We are important to somebody, be he friend, parent, husband, or wife. To feel that no one cares what we do, say, or accomplish is to invite a personality complex. A feeling of not being wanted might be the result of our own shortcoming by not being friendly and co-operative with others. It is generally true that if we are interested in other people they will be interested in us. God gave every person talents and responsibilities. To feel we have no abilities and no friends is to admit we do not want to use our abilities and make friends.

Can We Talk Things Over?

Marriage is complex and creates many situations that need sympathetic understanding. The wife, tired by the cares and problems of the children, a breakdown of the washer, and many other little irritating things that come up in a day, needs to be able to talk her problems over with her husband. He must be not only an outlet for her troubles, but also an aid in constructive advice and help. Likewise, the husband who has had a hard day at the office or in the factory needs a wife who will be understanding and afford him the opportunity to air his problems. Home is a place where husband and wife should feel free to "let down their hair." No home is able to keep everything running smoothly all the time, nor is that important. What is important for young people to consider is whether or not they have the capacity, the will, and the skill to talk things over rationally and without undue emotional involvement. The ability to talk things over before marriage is a good indication of how successful you will be in talking things over after marriage. A prospective husband or wife who is not willing to face realities and discuss problems is a poor marriage risk.

Attitude Toward Sex

In selecting a marriage mate you should give careful consideration to whether your prospective partner will meet with your approval with respect to your sex behavior. It is highly desirable to know the anatomy and physiology of the sex organs, but it is more important to understand what you and your partner think and do about sex. Sharing and growing together in this area, the most intimate of all human relationships, may spell success or failure in marriage. People who consider sex as the only important thing in marriage underestimate the other areas which are essential to marriage success. Sex is recognized as being psychological as well as physical. A person whose thinking is radically different from yours as to what sex is and should express will not satisfy your concept of sex. Knowledge of how your intended husband or wife feels about sex can be acquired in the normal association of dating and engagement. The mechanics and techniques of sex can be learned after marriage; but the sexual satisfaction hoped for in marriage can be achieved only when before marriage there is harmony and agreement as to what sex is and should mean to oneself and the partner.

Influences of Location and Occupation

The location in which people live and the occupation they follow are in some instances influential in aiding or hindering marriage opportunities. In an industrial area the number of men in any given location is high in proportion to the normal distribution. Women living in this area have the opportunity of meeting more men than they have in an area where employment calls for an abnormal concentration of women. To some extent this unbalanced ratio of men and women is true of some colleges. In engineering colleges there are more men than women; on the other hand, in schools of education women outnumber men.

Unbalanced ratios occur in some occupations. A woman grade-school teacher will likely find that the number of men teaching in the elementary school is relatively small. People living in areas where the ratios are unequal will find it advantageous to meet people of the opposite sex by belonging to young people's organizations of the church, joining clubs, and participating in civic and social activities.

What You Have to Offer

What *you* have to offer as a marriage partner is an important factor in determining *whom* you can get as a partner. To expect to attract a person with good character, education, stability, and ambition, you yourself must have these qualities. It may seem unromantic and businesslike to imply that seeking a marriage partner resembles shopping, but in reality there is much similarity. Unlike shopping, however, good husbands and wives are not found on the bargain counter.

Before Engagement Check List

If you are seriously considering engagement, the following check list will be of help:

1. Is it real love or infatuation?

2. Are our goals similar enough to work together in harmony?

3. Have we had disagreements and do we know how to resolve differences in an adult and Christian manner?

4. Do we agree on the majority of our interests, likes, and dislikes?

5. Do our parents agree we are ready for marriage? Do we have their approval?

6. Do my parents think well of the parents of the person I intend to marry?

7. Do we share the same faith and agree on how active and devoted we should be in the practice of that faith?

8. Are we accustomed to approximately the same standard of living?

9. If we become engaged, will we earnestly try to know each other better?

10. Do we consider engagements a serious and mature responsibility?

11. Have our friends, or some other influence, been instrumental in causing us to consider engagement before we are really ready?

12. Do I truly believe that the person whom I am seriously considering is the one who can and will fulfill my basic desires in marriage?

13. Are the misgivings I have about the one I love real or imaginary?

14. Are we good companions?

15. Do my friends think well of the one I love?

16. Do we really enjoy being together and doing things together without the stimulus of petting?

17. Are we willing and able to live on the income of the husband alone, even though both may plan to work after marriage?

18. If we are both in our teens, do we realize there will be a change in our interests, maturity, and activities when we reach our twenties? Will we then have as much in common as we now have?

Now We Are Engaged

Engagement, measured in terms of time, signifies that marriage is but a short distance away. It is your last chance to find out if you are as much in love as you think you are. Do you know, and does the one to whom you are engaged know, what being married will mean to both of you? Now that engagement is a reality and the competition of the dating days is over, it is time to discuss with all seriousness the many things which need understanding and have as yet not been solved. Are we in agreement on how long our engagement should be? To what extent, if any, should our standards and behavior patterns be relaxed? How much should I reveal of my past? Do I want to know all of my partner's past, or will some things, if revealed, be detrimental to our engagement and future? Does being engaged create a "we" feeling that was not present during dating days?

Being engaged is not just something to which one conforms socially to get publicity and to have a good time entertaining and being entertained. A proper engagement is a solemn promise made by a man and a woman to each other to become husband and wife in marriage. Such a promise should neither be lightly made nor easily broken. To be engaged, however, does not always mean that marriage will follow. It is estimated that approximately one third of all engagements are broken. This would indicate that during the period of engagement much is revealed that was not known before. Breaking an engagement has complications. However, if it is evident that only negative results can be expected from the marriage, the engagement had better be broken. The disappointments of a broken engagement are minor in comparison with a disastrous marriage or tragic divorce.

Meaning of Engagement to the Man

Men and women do not react to engagement in the same way. To the man, the engagement lacks the glamour and excitement enjoyed by women, yet there is much he needs to find out and do. Engagement is his opportunity to become better acquainted with his fiancée's parents; he must accurately evaluate how he is accepted by them. Does he share the feeling of being one of the family, or does he sense traces of coolness? Must every word and action be guarded, or can he be his natural self? The man must know and understand how his fiancée's parents live, the social and moral standards they maintain, and their concept of family life. Are their standards and concepts in accord with the way he wants and can afford to live? He must realize that his wife-to-be has been influenced by her parents' way of life, and this way has, in some degree, become a part of her. Engagement is the time for the man to see his "intended" as she really is — without make-up and in everyday work clothes. This is also the time for him to sample her cooking and observe her ideas on how to keep house. Certainly the man should know his engaged partner's feelings about such things as children, religion, money, working after marriage, place to live, etc. Serious disagreements on two or three of the above-mentioned items should be sufficient warning that a re-evaluation is advisable.

Meaning of Engagement to the Woman

If engagement seems to be definitely in the offing, the woman should realize that she is about to have her last chance to seriously weigh her fiancé in terms of what she really wants and expects of a husband. This decision is now hers to make; parents and friends may influence, but the final decision must be hers. She will want to find out how her future husband feels about money and its management. Will she be able to share in its management or will he make all decisions? Does she know his yearly income and the possibilities of job advancement in the future? Does he stay within the limits of his income, or will married life be a game of keeping one step ahead of the loan companies? Has his attitude on sex changed as the romance progressed? Are demands being made now that were not made during earlier dating? Does he assume liberties which are acceptable only after marriage, or does the experience and intimacy of the approaching engagement create a "we" feeling of respect and pride that is more sincere than ever before? Does the word mother-in-law make you shudder? Will your prospective in-laws accept you as a daughter or will they just "tolerate" you? Finally, does your man think as you do concerning your religious beliefs? Is going to Sunday school and church a waste of time to him? Will the yearly pledge for the financial support of the church be given cheerfully, or does the monthly payment on the car take precedence? Being able to worship together in harmony and understanding makes for a family solidarity not obtainable in any other way. It is evident by now that engagement is more than a round of showers, parties, and receiving congratulations and well-wishes. These pleasant experiences are not to be minimized, but after the excitement is over and marriage is a reality, will you be satisfied you have chosen wisely?

Engagement Symbols

The question of a ring is of interest to most young people considering engagement. Some feel that nothing in the way of a ring, fraternity pin, or other symbol is necessary to signify their engagement. Those who have this feeling say that money spent on a ring might better be used to buy furniture or some household appliance. This thinking is certainly not to be ridiculed. If the man and the woman both agree that this is the thing they wish to do, that is all that matters. A point not to be overlooked, however, is that the giving of a ring is an accepted and common practice of the majority of engaged couples. A ring may not seem important at the time of engagement, but a ring given after marriage does not have the same sentiment and meaning as one given for engagement. An electric range may be substituted for a ring, but it can never take its place in sentiment and in the "we" feeling expressed in a ring. If a man decides he would like to give a ring for engagement, should he give it as a surprise or would it be better if he and his fiancée selected it together? If he chooses a ring by himself, will his choice of price and design be in accordance with what his fiancée would want and be happy to wear? Most certainly a girl will be pleased to accept any ring which expressed the man's love, yet it might be better if both shared in the selection. It would then represent the best in expression and appreciation for both.

Length of Engagement

How long should an engagement be? When is an engagement too short, and when is it too long? Some authorities [2] on marriage and family life believe that there is a positive relationship between length of engagement and happiness in marriage. Longer engagements favor satisfactory marital adjustments. Engagements of six months' or less duration indicate 87 per cent with fair to poor adjustment. Engagements of two or more years indicate 55 per cent have fair to good adjustments. It should not be construed, however, that the longer the engagement, the better the adjustment. In fact, too long an engagement builds up tensions which may lead to frustrations. Too long an engagement may also resolve into a kind of substitute for marriage itself. There is no set formula for the length of an engagement. Couples living within the same block all of their life certainly know each other and their families better than the couple who were complete strangers until the time of dating. An engagement is long enough when the couple is satisfied that their problems, doubts, and misgivings are solved, and agree that marriage is a good risk.

Skeletons in the Closet

When two people planning on getting married have a past which is an open book for each to read, it is a wonderful foundation on which to build. Unfortunately, this is not always the case. For those who have some questionable experience in the past, the problem arises whether or not this experience should be re-

---

[2] E. W. Burgess and L. S. Cottrell, *Predicting Success or Failure in Marriage.* — Lewis M. Terman and Associates, *Psychological Factor in Marriage Happiness.*

vealed. For some, revealing the past is best; in other cases, it might create a chasm of doubt that can never be bridged. Some things, however, must be revealed if a marriage is to have a chance for success. Such things as a former marriage, a prison term, a large, burdensome debt, a serious physical abnormality, or anything that might constitute a definite threat to the marriage if it is not known in advance, should be told. Many engagements are broken when something is revealed that is unacceptable to the engaged partner. In fact, if during the period of engagement one or both of the couple feel differently toward each other than at the time of engagement, they should seriously reevaluate their relationship. Engagement must stand up under the close scrutiny of either partner. The intimacy experienced in engagement brings out traits and characteristics not suspected in the dating stage. This closer association might reveal a weak character trait, an inferiority complex, or any unknown number of things that will create a stumbling block for a happy marriage. Engagement is no time for make-believe or deception — only true selves must be expressed. If what each finds in the other is good and fits the ideals and concepts of both, marriage will prove to be the most wonderful and satisfying experience in life. However, if they discover that they are decidedly and irremediably incompatible, the prospects for future happiness are dim and highly doubtful.

Check List for Engaged Couples

1. Have we reached a satisfactory agreement relative to our religious beliefs and church activity?

2. Are we in harmony concerning money matters?

Following are some topics involving money on which there should be agreement: (a) Keeping a budget; (b) Amount of money that should be saved; (c) Who will manage the money; (d) Should the wife work? (e) What furniture and appliances are essential to begin with? (f) Standard of living relative to amount spent for rent or payment on a home.

3. Do we have a mutual interest in recreational activities?

4. Are we in agreement on the question of birth control and size of family?

5. Are we in harmony as to our thinking on the subject of sex?

6. Have our prospective in-laws accepted us and our families?

7. Have we reached agreement on personal habits and social practices, such as drinking and smoking?

8. If we are in our teens, have we proved to our parents, minister, and friends that we are mature enough to assume the responsibilities of married life?

9. Do we understand each other's social, economic, and educational ambitions?

10. Have both of us had a complete physical examination and are we prepared to enter marriage in the best possible health?

11. Are we familiar with and ready to live up to the promises given in the marriage vows?

Mixed Marriages

In reality all marriages are mixed marriages. The degree to which the marriage is mixed has much to do with the success of the marriage. Marked differences in education, intelligence, social background, age, physical stature, health, race, religion, etc., may cause misunderstandings serious enough to cause the marriage to fail. Some of these differences are less important than others, but the one given special emphasis in this discussion relates to religion.

Religion is interpreted by different people in different ways — all sincere in the conviction of their beliefs. We in the United States are blessed with the privilege of worshiping in the religion of our choice. When we make this choice, it carries with it the responsibilities of doing what is in our power and capabilities to further the work of our church. In marriage it is very desirable that husband and wife be in agreement regarding their religion so they can grow together in their faith and guide their children in religious education. When husband and wife are of different faiths, this growth cannot come about effectively. Fundamental differences in concepts and practices exist among Roman Catholics, Protestants, and Jews. Even among some Protestant denominations enough major differences exist to cause tensions between husband and wife if each is of a different faith. One denomination may be very strict in expecting its members to attend church regularly and frequently; it may be opposed to dancing, playing cards, or the use of alcohol in any form. Another denomination may be quite liberal in all of these issues. Some denominations encourage their members to interpret religion according to what each individual member thinks and rationalizes for himself, while other denominations follow strictly the wording of the Bible and adhere to a form of worship established by a governing body of the church. Differences such as these are difficult, if not impossible, to reconcile. It is possible that man and wife of the same denomination can have serious religious disagreements on such issues as how regularly they should attend church, the amount of money to pledge for its support, and how active they should be in church organizations. The wife may feel, and rightly so, that Sunday morning should be reserved for church, but the husband insists that golf is more important to him and that he must have the use of the family car. The wife may get up early on Sunday to get the children ready for Sunday school, but the husband feels Sunday is his only day to relax and catch up on much-needed sleep. In general, however, the issues between husband and wife of the same denomination are not so serious that they cannot be resolved. When, however, the differences in belief of husband and wife involve the fundamentals of what to believe and how faith should be practiced, as is the case between Protestants and Roman Catholics, the difficulties to be overcome are serious indeed. In such cases the sincerity and depth of feeling that husband and wife each have for their religion largely determines the degree of acceptance of one another's faith. The stronger each is in his convictions the more difficult will be the situation.

Judson T. Landis, in a study comparing the divorce rates in marriages of people of mixed, non-mixed, and no religious affiliation, indicates that when the religion of husband and wife is the same, the divorce rate for Roman Catholics is 4.4 per cent, Jews 5.2 per cent, and Protestants 6.0 per cent. The Roman Catholic Church does not recognize divorce. Roman Catholics do, however, recognize separation instead of divorce. Separation is less frequent among Protestants or Jews. Landis further points out that it is significant that the divorce rate is 17.9 per cent when neither husband nor wife professes any religion.[3]

In religious belief and practice, father and mother do not have the same influence on their children. Mother proves to be the dominating influence according to a study by Landis which shows that 75 per cent of the girls and 65 per cent of the boys follow their mother's faith. He further concludes that the divorce rate is 20.6 per cent in mixed marriages where the father is Roman Catholic and the mother is Protestant. In a home where the father is Roman Catholic, he will insist that the children be reared in his church; but if the mother is Protestant, and the dominating influence, the children will follow her religion, especially if she is firm in her faith. The end result in either case is confusion and discord, both for parents and children.

Marriages of mixed religious beliefs are of major concern to both Protestants and Roman Catholics. John L. Thomas, S. J., of the Department of Sociology, St. Louis University, has this to say regarding valid and invalid mixed marriages: "During the decade 1940 to 1950, valid mixed marriages accounted for between 25 and 30 per cent of all Catholic marriages."[4] Concerning invalid marriages he states, "The Bishop's Committee estimated that each year between 15 and 25 per cent of all marriages involving Catholics were invalid." On the basis of these figures between 40 and 50 per cent of Catholics are involved in mixed marriages.

---

[3] Judson T. Landis and Mary G. Landis, *Building a Successful Marriage*, 3d ed., 1958.

[4] John L. Thomas, S. J., *The American Catholic Family*, 1956.

Unfortunately, when people are young and very much in love, the religious issue seems to be no major hurdle. If one or the other does not want to change his faith, they see little difficulty in each going his own way. Religious faith, however, is deep-seated, especially if in early training and education it was given strong emphasis by the parents. Husband and wife going their own religious way not only creates home problems but is very confusing and distracting to their children. Parents take for granted that they will give their children the best education possible, and they make real sacrifices to give them a good home and the necessary social training, but a good religious training is even more important. The Bible asks this question of people who place material things above all else: "For what is a man profited, if he shall gain the whole world, and lose his own soul? or what shall a man give in exchange for his soul?" (Matthew 16:26)

Protestants who are contemplating marriage with a Roman Catholic must realize the fundamental and deep-seated differences that exist between them. Here are some issues which arise:

1. The Roman Catholic Church insists that the marriage ceremony must be performed by a priest, even though the Protestant wants to be married by his or her minister.

2. The Roman Catholic Church further requires that all children of the couple must be reared in the Roman Catholic faith and that the Protestant parent will in no way interfere with the children's religious and parochial school education. This is an impossible thing to do for a Protestant who is strong in faith and has the conviction that his or her faith is in closer agreement with the Bible than is the Roman Catholic faith.

The antenuptial agreement, which must be signed by both the Catholic and the non-Catholic partner when the marriage is performed by a Catholic priest, stipulates the following requirements:

NON-CATHOLIC PARTY

I, the undersigned _____ of
_____, not a member of the Catholic Church, desiring to contract marriage with _____
_____ of _____,
who is a member of the Catholic Church, propose to do so with the understanding that the marriage bond thus contracted can be broken only by death.

And thereupon in consideration of such marriage, I, the said _____, do hereby covenant, promise, and agree to and with the said _____ that he (she), the said _____, shall be permitted the free exercise of religion according to the Catholic faith without hinderance or adverse comment and that all the children of either sex born of such marriage shall be baptized and educated only in the faith and according to the teachings of the Roman Catholic Church, even if the said _____ shall die first.

I hereby promise that no other marriage ceremony than that by the Catholic priest shall take place.

I furthermore realize the holiness of the use of marriage according to the teaching of the Catholic Church, which condemns birth control and similar abuses of marriage. I shall have due respect for the religious principles and convictions of my Catholic partner.

Witness my hand this .... day of ...., 19........,
at _____ in the County of _____,
and State of _____.
Signed in the presence of
Rev. _____   _____

Signature of non-Catholic

CATHOLIC PARTY

I, the undersigned _____, a member of the Catholic Church, of _____ Parish,
_____, wishing to contract marriage with

...., a non-Catholic, hereby
solemnly promise to have all the children of either sex
born of this marriage baptized and reared only in the
Catholic faith. Furthermore, I promise that no other
marriage ceremony than that by the Catholic priest shall
take place. I also realize my obligation in conscience
to practice my religion faithfully and prudently to en-
deavor by prayer, good example, and the reception of
the Sacraments to induce my life partner to investigate
seriously the teachings of the Catholic Church in the
hope that such investigation may lead to conversion.
Witness my hand this _____ day of _____, 19___,
at _____ in the County of _____,
and State of _____.
Signed in the presence of
Rev. _____   _____

                          Signature of Catholic

3. Birth control is a source of friction in a mixed
marriage. Most Protestant churches have taken no firm
stand for or against birth control, and many Protestant
church members apparently practice birth control by
some mechanical or chemical means. The Roman Catholic Church does not sanction such means of regulating
the size of a family. It sanctions the "rhythm method"
of birth control. This method seeks to establish the time
the ovum is in the Fallopian tube, and the couple re-
frains from sex relations during this period. Assuming
that the Protestant partner does consent to the "rhythm
method," or the Roman Catholic to the mechanical
method, early religious training and social pressures
may nevertheless lead to serious disagreements or
frustrations.

4. Mixed marriages also create a problem involving
in-laws. In a mixed marriage the couple themselves
may be in agreement concerning their religious practices, but this agreement may not be shared by their
in-laws. Even after marriage there is some parental in-

fluence, and when this influence exerts opposing pressures on the couple, it creates family trouble.

5. The Roman Catholic Church does not recognize divorce. By special dispensation the marriage partner can procure a separation; but in a separation the state does not give consent to remarry.

6. In a mixed marriage, husband and wife frequently become weak in their own faith and eventually do not attend church at all.

7. The children of mixed marriages are torn between their loyalties to their parents. When children become old enough to reason and think for themselves, it is difficult for them to understand why going to church with one parent is forbidden. Children love both parents and are loyal to both in all areas except religion. They cannot understand why they should share one faith and not the other, and why mother and father seem to agree on all things except religion.

Jewish and Gentile mixed marriages also have many difficulties. Not only is there a vast difference in religion, but racial and family traditions are in such contrast that a mixed marriage of this kind is difficult indeed.

What Is the Answer?

Previous discussions indicated that the selection of a mate involves many factors, religion being an important one. A realistic understanding of what is involved in a mixed religious marriage is necessary if a couple is to understand the probability of success or failure in marriage. A Protestant, strong in his or her faith, will not comply with the demands made by the Roman Catholic Church; and a Roman Catholic, strong in faith, will not give in to the demand of the Protestant.

We have religious freedom in this country, and we should respect religious faiths other than our own, but we need not subscribe to principles of faith contrary to our convictions. When two people of conflicting religious views are considering marriage, they must be frank and realistic with each other. If they cannot agree on religion, it is best that they part as friends and look for someone who is in harmony with their thinking. To get married and live in disagreement and strife is certainly not desirable. Faith should be a uniting force in a family, not a dividing one. Maintaining a strong faith has enough competition without the difficulties created by mixed religions.

Your Minister and Your Doctor

It may seem strange to include both the minister and the doctor in the same category, yet each plays an important role in your life before you say "I do" in the marriage ceremony. You will want to know your minister well. His responsibility is not just preaching, marrying couples, and burying the dead, but, in addition, he is one to whom you can go for guidance and advice. Your minister is well trained by education and experience as a counselor and adviser. He has married many couples, baptized their children, and, in some instances, has watched these children go to grade school, high school, and college. He has shared with them the joys of their home and comforted them in their sorrows. He has counseled with those whose marriage developed undue stresses and strains, but he has also learned the ways of good family life from those in his congregation who have celebrated fifty years of happy married life. Your minister is a friend who not only can bring you his personal experience and advice, but he can also help you to maintain faith, the foundation upon which a Christian marriage is built.. Your minister is your friend. Consult him.

Your doctor is also your friend; he, too, is a good counselor and a good adviser. You will want to know him, for his skill in maintaining health and for the many ways he can give advice concerning the physical and mental problems arising out of marriage and everyday living. You will want to go to him for a thorough examination before marriage. It is only fair that you begin your married life with as strong and healthy a body as is possible for you to have. You will want to talk to your doctor concerning sex and to clear up any misinformation or misgivings you may have. Your doctor can be trusted to give you advice that is to your best interest.

Early Marriages

Understanding and appreciating the requirements of what makes for a successful marriage is commendable, but of equal, if not of more importance, is the realization that social and chronological maturity are a must. As indicated by the following data, the trend toward marrying in the teens is increasing.

In 1940, 1.4 per cent of the men who married were under twenty years of age; this rose to 2.1 per cent in 1951. In 1940, 9.8 per cent of the women who married were under twenty years of age; in 1951 this rose to 13.7 per cent.[5] There is little doubt that these percentages are still rising. Is there any reason why early

---

[5] Lester Kirkendall, *Too Young to Marry*. New York: Public Affairs Committee, Pamphlet 236.

marriages fail when young people have enthusiasm, physical vigor, and a determination to conquer the world? In many cases teen-age marriages have succeeded; but statistical evidence clearly indicates the percentage of successful early marriages is definitely lower than that of marriages of more mature people.

Why Do Marriages of Young People Fail?

Marriage success is closely related to, and affected by, the economic situation of the couple. When work is plentiful and pay is good, young people feel they can get married and "make a go of it." The young wife can find employment, and with their double income the two can live in comfort, if not luxury. On the surface it sounds practicable, but "all is not gold that glitters." When the wife works, it soon becomes apparent that not all earnings are profit, for extra clothing, food, and taxes take a sizable amount of money. Another economic problem not always calculated by the young couple is pregnancy. Generally speaking, a young husband does not earn high wages, and the wife's pregnancy sets off a chain of unexpected events. Not only must the wife give up her job, but other adjustments must be made because of decreased income and increased expenses. Social activities must be curtailed, and the standard of living must be lowered. This may mean renting in a less desirable neighborhood. Such circumstances, which were not anticipated or contemplated during the courtship under the full moon of last summer, may result in irritations and discord.

Social pressure sometimes persuades teen-agers to marry. A girl in high school may belong to a club in which her club sisters are either getting married or becoming engaged. As her single friends become fewer and fewer, she too feels the need of "joining the parade" of marriages. Instead of making new friends through new associations, she assumes that marriage will solve her problems.

Another common pressure for getting married young is the misconception that when a woman reaches her mid-twenties she is approaching the status of an "old maid." She may also be troubled by the fear that there is something about her that makes her unattractive to men.

To some extent the military service lowers the marriage age. Couples must decide whether to marry before the young man enters military service or wait until he returns. The girl may feel that if she waits she is taking a chance of losing to the competition of other girls her boy friend will meet while away. Then, too, she feels that by the time he returns she may be too old to find someone else if he has changed his mind about her during his service. If the young couple marries before the man has had his military service, there is always the possibility of the woman's becoming pregnant during this brief time of marriage; and this situation complicates matters when the man has to leave. Whether the couple marries or not, during the period of military service there will be several years of separation. Being separated creates situations where both will change because of different environments. The man will be meeting new people and doing a lot of traveling, while the woman remains at home. Because of the vast difference in their experiences, the man will probably change more than the woman. In the late teens and early twenties there is also a change of maturity. With the change of environment and the change in maturity taking place during military separation, the couple may almost be like strangers when they are again united. Whether to marry before or after military service should be given careful consideration.

Family tensions at home cause some people to marry young. Conflicts with parents become irritating to the point where it is felt that getting married and leading an independent life is the best solution for avoiding the control exercised by mother and father. All too often this action is like jumping from the "frying pan into the fire." A person who is not mature enough to tolerate some irritating home situations is probably not mature enough to take on the adult role of husband or wife. Young people whose marriage is induced by escape motives reflect immaturity and lack the understanding of what marriage is all about.

When teen-agers "go steady" too long with one person, they have a tendency to become "serious" and so involved that they marry before they reach a mature age for marriage. When the world has narrowed to one friend and marriage becomes the main goal while yet in high school, serious thought must be given as to whether marriage is the right answer to the problem. School may be unattractive for one reason or another to the teen-ager, but marriage does not solve the difficulty. In fact, marriage will be substituting a more serious problem for what is now a relatively minor one.

Lester Kirkendall lists some excellent "Go Slow" signs if an early marriage is contemplated.

1. "Go Slow when there is a feeling that it is get married now or never." Marriage does not have this urgency. If it does, something is not in accord with the normal and accepted pattern of marriage.

2. "Go Slow when there is a one-sided feeling." If one person is eager to get married and the other indifferent about marriage, it certainly indicates that they are not thinking in terms of "we" and are not doing and acting like a couple with a unified purpose.

3. "Go Slow when there are strong parental objections." There are isolated instances where the parent is wrong in objecting to a marriage. Objections raised by the vast majority of parents are usually based on sound reasoning and their own experience. Most parents will sacrifice for their children much beyond their parental responsibility, for they want to see their children happy and well-adjusted also in marriage. Parents know what it takes to make a marriage succeed. Some young couples whose parents object to their marriage sometimes take the attitude, "We are marrying each other, not our parents." In a sense this is true, but only in part. A young couple can be independent of their parents to a certain degree, but how much more pleasant and complete their marriage would be if they had the suggestions, help, and good wishes of their parents.

4. "Go Slow when there is a pregnancy." As stated many times before, there is no substitute for the love and behavior before marriage that eliminates the possibility of pregnancy. However, the temptation to error is ever present, and people sometimes yield to sin. When pregnancy does occur to an unmarried couple, it is only natural that the question of marriage arises. Each case must be judged separately. However, there are a few general suggestions which can be considered. If the couple is engaged and planning to marry in the future, the best solution is marriage. If the couple has

94

reached the stage of engagement, they most likely have given marriage enough thought to sincerely want their marriage to succeed, even though it is by the compulsion of circumstances.

What about the couple who are not in love and who apparently are not suited for each other? A couple in this situation needs professional advice, either from their minister, a family service agency, or someone else who is trained in marriage counseling. The course of action to follow must be to make as good a situation as possible out of a bad one. Under no circumstances should abortion be considered — it is sinful and completely unsatisfactory. Abortion in this case is murder, and to murder is a gross sin. The unborn child had no part in the way it is conceived; but as soon as life begins, it has every right to be born under the best circumstances possible. One acceptable solution might be for the parents of the pregnant girl to rear the child and give it the love and affection needed. This arrangement would free the mother to work and be with the child in her parental home. Much depends upon the attitude and circumstances of the girl's parents. Another solution would be for a child welfare agency to care for the child, in which case the mother could give partial support until she marries or is able to care for her child. In some cases it might be best to have a child welfare agency find a good home for the child's adoption. If the couple feels they should marry for the sake of giving the child a legal name, although they know full well they cannot be compatible, they should explore every possible solution before entering a marriage which will likely end in divorce.[6]

---

[6] Quotations only from Lester Kirkendall, *Too Young to Marry*. See fn. 5.

The Marriage Ceremony

The marriage ceremony is beautiful, sacred, and serious. To think of marriage and enter into it in any other way is to make mockery of the very foundation upon which family life and the culture of civilization rests. Marriage is not only of interest to the two people getting married, but to the church and state as well. The state is concerned enough to have made some legal requirements. The couple must be of legal age, have a blood test (in some states), and satisfy certain requisites relative to close blood relationship. A marriage becomes a legal contract that can be dissolved only through court action. The state is interested in protecting the legal rights of those being married and of the children that result from the marriage.

The church is interested in marriage because marriage was instituted by God. It is an estate ordained by God in which a man and a woman are to live together as one. It is intended to be for life and should therefore not be broken.

The following wedding ceremony is one type used in the Lutheran Church. It is similar to the ceremony generally used in Protestant churches. Read and study it carefully with the view of grasping its full signficance.

THE ORDER OF A MARRIAGE (Lutheran)

A Short Form

❡ The persons to be married having presented themselves at the entrance of the chancel, the man on the right hand and the woman on his left, the Minister shall say:

Dearly Beloved: We are assembled here in the presence of God and these witnesses to join together this man and this woman in holy matrimony, which was instituted by God for the welfare and happiness of mankind, blessed by our Lord Jesus Christ, and likened by St. Paul to the mystical union subsisting between Christ and His Church, and which is to be held in honor among all men. Wherefore those who purpose to enter this holy estate should do so with a profound sense of the seriousness of the obligations they are about to assume, duly and devoutly weighing what Holy Scripture teaches concerning husbands and wives, and bearing in mind that the vow and covenant once made may not be broken. Our Savior has declared that a man shall forsake his father and mother and cleave unto his wife, for they twain shall be one flesh. By His Apostles He has instructed those who enter into wedlock to cherish mutual esteem and love; to bear with each other's infirmities and weaknesses; to comfort each other in sickness, trouble, and sorrow; in honesty and industry to provide for each other and for their household in temporal things; to pray for and encourage each other in the things which pertain to God; and to live together as the heirs of the grace of life.

These two persons have come hither to be made one in this holy estate. If there be any here present who can show just cause why they may not lawfully be joined in marriage, let him now speak or ever after hold his peace.

Forasmuch, then, as nothing has been shown to hinder this marriage, I ask you:

N., wilt thou have N., here present, to be thy wedded wife, to live together after God's ordinance in the holy estate of matrimony? Wilt thou love her, comfort her, honor her, and keep her in sickness and in health, and, forsaking all others, keep thee only unto her so long as ye both shall live?

I will.

N., wilt thou have N., here present, to be thy wedded husband, to live together after God's ordinance in the holy estate of matrimony? Wilt thou love him, comfort him, honor and obey him, and keep him in sickness and in health, and, forsaking all others, keep thee only unto him so long as ye both shall live?

I will.

❡ Then the Minister may say:
Who giveth this woman to be married to this man?

❡ Then the father or another relative shall say:
I do.

❡ The father or another relative of the woman shall with
his right hand put her right hand into the right hand of
the Minister, who shall cause the man with his right hand
to take the woman by her right hand and to say after him
as they face each other:

I, N., in the presence of God and this assembly, / take
thee, N., to be my wedded wife, / and plight thee my
troth in every duty, / not to part from thee / till death
us do part.

❡ Then shall they loose their right hands. Then shall the
Minister with his right hand cause the woman with her
right hand to take the man by his right hand and shall
likewise say after the Minister:

I, N., in the presence of God and this assembly, / take
thee, N., to be my wedded husband, / and plight thee my
troth in every duty, / not to part from thee / till death
us do part.

❡ Then shall they again loose their right hands, and if
the wedding ring be used, the Minister shall now ask for
it and say:

In token of your vows thus mutually plighted, you N.
give, and you, N., receive the wedding ring.

❡ Then the Minister, taking the ring with his right hand
shall deliver it to the man, who shall then put it on the
fourth finger of the woman's left hand, and the Minister
shall say, and the man shall say after him:

Receive this ring / as a pledge and token / of wedded
love and faithfulness.

❡ Or:

With this ring I thee wed, N., / in the name of the Father
and of the Son and of the Holy Ghost, Amen.

❡ Then shall the minister say:

Join your right hands.

❡ Then shall the Minister lay his right hand upon the
hands and say:

Forasmuch as N. and N. have consented together in holy
wedlock and have witnessed the same before God and
this assembly (these witnesses) (and thereto have given
and pledged their troth, each to the other), and have
declared the same (by giving and receiving a ring, and

by joining hands: I pronounce them husband and wife in the name of the Father and of the Son and of the Holy Ghost. Amen.

What, therefore, God hath joined together let not man put asunder.

℄ Then shall the persons married kneel for prayer, and the Minister shall say:

O Eternal God, Creator and Preserver of all mankind, Giver of all spiritual grace, the Author of everlasting life: send Thy blessing upon these Thy servants, this man and this woman, whom we bless in Thy name, that, living faithfully together, they may surely perform and keep the vow and covenant betwixt them made and may ever remain in perfect love and peace together, and so live in this life according to Thy laws that in the world to come they may have life everlasting; through Jesus Christ, our Lord.

Our Father who art in heaven. Hallowed be Thy name. Thy kingdom come. Thy will be done on earth as it is in heaven. Give us this day our daily bread. And forgive us our trespasses, as we forgive those who trespass against us. And lead us not into temptation. But deliver us from evil. For Thine is the kingdom and the power and the glory forever and ever. Amen.

℄ Then shall the Minister pronounce the Benediction:
The Lord bless thee and keep thee.
The Lord make His face shine upon thee and be gracious unto thee.
The Lord lift up His countenance upon thee and give thee peace. Amen.

The Honeymoon

Is a honeymoon really essential, and what purpose does it serve? The majority of newlyweds are in favor of a honeymoon. The honeymoon aids the couple to make the transition from single to married life under favorable conditions. Learning to be Mr. and Mrs. takes time. Getting more fully acquainted is best accomplished when the couple are free to do things as they choose, without being molested by the curiosity of friends and the interference of parents.

The honeymoon enables the couple to adjust to the intimacies now shared by each other. For the idealistic and sheltered woman the reality of living as man and wife may be difficult to accept. No longer is her room the shelter it used to be. She must learn the habits and reactions of a man, and she may find that his background and training lack the delicacy and sensitiveness that she has known. Sex relations now become a reality, and the kind of love, consideration, and response they have experienced will do much to start their sex life either as something fine and harmonious, or with fear and apprehension.

The honeymoon should be so planned that the couple can be at ease and have complete freedom to do as they choose. A honeymoon may consist of a trip abroad, a trip to Niagara Falls, some time at a resort, or a trip to a neighboring state. Where to go is important, but of more significance is that both agree on what they want to do and can enjoy together. It is a mistake for the couple to see how far they can travel and how many things they can see in a limited time. A race against time and energy defeats the purpose of the honeymoon; rest and relaxation are important for the recovery from the exciting weeks before the wedding.

The length of the honeymoon depends largely on how much time is available and the financial circumstances of the couple. A honeymoon on borrowed money is not advisable. By careful planning, many interesting things can be done and a number of places visited with little expense. A honeymoon costing several thousand dollars may have covered more miles, more pictures may have been taken, more and better hotels may have been enjoyed, and more publicity may have been given it in the paper, but it may not have served better than a moderate honeymoon in starting the marriage on the road to happiness.

What Married Life Means

When the struggle and competition of single life are over and marriage is a reality, the couple are now working as a team, thinking as a team, and sacrificing for a common goal. Marriage does not mean that individuality has been lost, but it does mean that what is said and done is of concern to both.

Much is said and read about the breakdown of the family, but the fact still remains that most marriages are happy and well adjusted. Married life has no mysterious or secret formula for its success, but it does need the earnest desire of husband and wife to succeed. It is important to realize that, although differences of opinion and disagreements will occur, these can be solved within the framework of love, understanding, and forgiveness. Millions of people have been successfully married; to ignore their experiences and advice would be foolhardy indeed.

Landis and Landis, who are authorities on the subject of family living, list seven areas in which married couples should have a workable agreement:[7]

1. Money
2. In-Law Relationships
3. Sex Adjustments

[7] Judson T. Landis and Mary G. Landis, *Personal Adjustment, Marriage and Family Living.*

4. Social and Recreational Activities

5. Associating with Friends

6. Religious Adjustment

7. Training and Disciplining of Children

A complete treatise on each topic is not within the scope of this discussion. However, for the couple anticipating marriage, understanding the significance of each area is essential. These areas are the spokes in the wheel of marriage that will carry it to success or failure. Adjustments in these areas are not made immediately and are not always made with smoothness, but time, patience, and prayer are the "wonder drugs" that see most young couples through the crises. The expression "Rome was not built in a day" is an axiom well applied to marriage.

Money in Marriage

Money is not the root of all evil, but the misuse and mismanagement of it makes it rank in the forefront as one of the most difficult adjustments in marriage. The trouble is not so much in the amount of money earned, but in how it should be managed and for what it should be spent.

The value people place on money and material things stems from many influences. Here again the parental home sets much of the pattern. What mother and father consider important and for what purpose they spend their money has a profound influence on what their children think important and necessary. If money spent in the home is only for the necessities of shelter, furniture, food, and clothing; if something new in home appliances means shopping for the best wholesale buy, or shopping through the classified ads in the newspaper; if every dollar spent buys real value rather than extras and the latest designs and models, then the entire economic pattern of training is one of conservatism. If, in another type home, only the best is purchased in abundance, eating-out is customary, social functions are routine, vacations mean going to unusual places in the finest of style, things are purchased for the home without questions about price, but rather, what style it should be and how soon available, then this home represents training in abundance and luxury. Both of these ways of living are typical and respectable, and no criticism is implied. However, when marriage brings together two people from homes of decidedly different economic status and atmosphere, the probability of misunderstandings on money matters is great. Husband and wife should agree on values, where items should be bought, how they should be bought, and the purpose they should serve. A man or woman reared in a home where the pay check is just enough to supply the minimum comforts of living, learns to value money differently than the man or woman who comes from a home where the so-called necessities are, in reality, luxuries.

Who should have the major responsibility in handling money in the home, the husband or the wife? Should the husband bring home the pay check, turn it over to his wife, and let her apportion it to meet all obligations and, if possible, save a little? Is it better to cash the check and hide the money in a volume of the encyclopedia, as a common fund for both, or should the husband give his wife an allowance for running the home while he uses the balance of his pay as he deems necessary? No definite answer can be given as to how a specific couple should work out their money problems.

Each couple must work out a solution satisfactory to themselves. The methods that will work in one household will not work in another. However, one thing is important — husband and wife must agree on a plan. It would seem that the person better qualified for handling money should assume this responsibility, whether it be husband or wife. Jealousy or selfishness between husband and wife regarding money has no place in marriage.

A family has difficulty living harmoniously and efficiently when it does not use good judgment in the spending of money. Spending more money than is earned spells trouble. Keeping up with the Joneses may be barely possible, but even if their standard is reached, the Smiths will have an even higher standard. Each rung of the economic ladder becomes more difficult to climb. Money is a household word and a household problem. For a person contemplating marriage it is essential to know how the marriage partner feels about money and his or her capability of handling it.

In-Laws

In-laws are part of every family, and rightly so. In-laws can be a factor in either happiness or trouble. The younger the age of a couple at the time of marriage, the more probability that in-laws will interfere. When a wife is still young, it is natural for her mother to be vitally interested in her and to offer many suggestions. The new husband may resent this interest on the part of his wife's mother; but he himself may not realize that he is being influenced by his parents. He feels the help and advice given by his parents is equal to, or better than, that given by his mother-in-law and, as a result, friction develops. The longer the couple is married, the more in-law trouble tends to decrease. As time progresses, a better understanding and a give-and-take attitude on the part of the whole family solves most of the real and imaginary problems. By the time twenty years of married life have passed, there may be a complete reversal as to who gives advice and assistance. The parents of the husband or wife may be needing some type of help, or it might be necessary for them to live with one of their children. It is interesting to note that most of the in-law trouble lies between the women in the families; relatively little friction exists between men. Whether trouble between families is magnified or minimized depends on the attitude and willingness of all concerned to work out differences. The young couple should take seriously what they promised each other in their wedding vows, and in-laws should realize their role is one of well-meaning advice and guidance, not interference. Honest differences will occur in every family, but when the spirit of tolerance and love have real meaning, differences of opinion can be reconciled.

Sex Adjustment

Adjustment in this area is necessary for a happy marriage. When sex is rightly thought of and practiced, it is a powerful force for unity; when it is not held sacred, few marriages survive. Sex is not the only important phase of marriage, as so many young people imagine it to be, nor is it a magic isolated something that will make the marriage succeed in spite of everything else. For some people sex adjustment may be difficult; but it is good to know that the husband and wife who love, understand, and respect each other will in all probability become well adjusted also in this area. Sex is not a miracle cure for disagreements or maladjusted behavior patterns. A husband who comes home drunk, swears, beats his wife, and is a general nuisance, is not likely to find his wife very receptive to his sex advances. Likewise, a wife who is involved in too many social affairs and in interests other than her husband is likely to find his affection and interest in her diminishing. It takes time for newlyweds to learn to know each other in simple matters, such as the wife learning to bake her husband's favorite pie, or getting the starch just right in his shirt collar. But something so compelling and forceful yet delicate and emotional as sex requires even more time to learn and appreciate together. Approximately fifty per cent of young married couples make a successful sex adjustment early in marriage — for others a year or more may be necessary.

Social and Recreational Activities

Modern living has made the social and recreational aspect of family life increasingly important. The forty-hour week leaves much time for the family to spend together. How this time is spent is a problem to which every family needs to give serious consideration.

Recreation means different things to different people. Recreation should stimulate good physical and mental health, be socially acceptable, and be in the best interest of the family. To some people recreation means watching television, playing cards, gardening, playing golf, doing volunteer work for the Red Cross, pursuing a hobby, etc. Here is one bit of warning concerning so-called recreation. When recreation becomes so competitive that physical exhaustion and mental frustration is the result, it is no longer recreation. Golf can be played for fun and exercise; but it ceases to be recreation when the score becomes so mentally upsetting that all sense of values is lost. Playing bridge is excellent recreation, but when the prize is the goal, instead of fun, companionship, and relaxation, it is no longer recreation. The opportunities for recreation are numerous. Community centers, schools, churches, and clubs offer a variety of recreation for the whole family.

Association with Friends

Choosing friends is a major responsibility for every married couple. We are judged by the friends we keep. The husband has friends at work; the wife has friends in her club. But they need friends they can share together on a family basis. A young married couple might assume they are self-sufficient and can live unto themselves, but this is not true. Life soon becomes dull and uninteresting if friends do not share in creating new ideas and interests. True friends are not only good companions; they are also indispensable help in time of need. "A friend in need is a friend indeed."

Religious Adjustment

Phases of religion and family have been discussed previously. It is worth repeating, however, that married people need to make a good adjustment in this area from the beginning of marriage. Not only will going to church and worshiping together strengthen the relationship as husband and wife, but all problems of life will be solved more readily and satisfactorily if faith and religious principles are the basis for their solution. Love between husband and wife needs and wants to share that which is good and edifying. Religion satisfies this need. Worshiping, praying, and working to-

107

gether with unity of purpose serves like a cementing force in marriage. The family that prays together stays together.

Training and Discipline of Children

To the young married couple child training seems of no immediate concern, but the way they live will have a direct bearing on how they rear their children. A child is the greatest gift that can come to husband and wife, and as they together love and lovingly care for their precious baby, they will share one of life's finest joys.

To know what is best in training and discipline for children is not easy, but the responsibility cannot be evaded. Children are pliable, and they are shaped by the gentle and not so gentle forces of their environment. When these forces are love and devotion, and give a child a feeling of being wanted, they make for normal growth and behavior. Children learn by observation and experience. One form of learning may involve punishment by the parents. Punishment seems to be the only thing some parents practice, and others completely avoid it. What is a practical and realistic approach to punishment? A child must learn that punishment of some kind follows wrongdoing. A teen-age boy learns by sad experience that driving an automobile around a curve faster than the law of centrifugal force permits results in an accident. A child who disobeys a parent's warning not to touch a hot stove will suffer immediate and impressive consequences.

Children can learn discipline by experience, but some experiences are too severe to be learned in this way. A child must be taught the danger of playing with a gun; to learn by experience that a loaded gun kills is obviously out of the question. A child that does things it should not do needs correction — assuming, of course, the parent had earlier given adequate training and advice. Some children are best corrected by reasoning with them, while for others the denial or withdrawal of privileges is more effective. Some children respond to scolding while others seem only to understand spanking. Whatever is done should not be done in a fit of anger or in a spirit of revenge. Children do not resent punishment if they know mother and father love them and that the punishment was administered for their good. Punishment ought to be used as a device for teaching. When the punishment causes the child to be more resentful and disobedient, it may be advisable to modify the type of corrective measure.

Parents should agree on discipline. One parent cannot be the sole disciplinarian, for that practice precludes joint responsibility, and it puts the punishing parent in a bad light with the child. Knowing how to discipline is one of the great challenges to parents. It can be rewarding in satisfaction and pride when the child grows to maturity as a well-disciplined and integrated person, increasing "in wisdom and stature, and in favor with God and man." (Luke 2:52)

Conclusion

Traveling the road of life from teen-age and courtship to marriage and family is an interesting and challenging experience, filled with joys and sorrows, achievements and disappointments. The teen-age miles of the road of life should not only be happy ones as such, but they should at the same time be a preparation for the years that lie ahead. The slogan of an insurance company reminds us of the importance of the fact that "the future belongs to those who prepare for it." What you do along the road of life in teen-age will to a large extent determine what the future will have in store for you. This gives to the teen-age added importance. In the teen-age years and throughout life you will be safe if you follow the maxim of the Psalmist: "Thy Word is a lamp unto my feet and a light unto my path." (Psalm 119:105)

WHAT TO READ

NOTE: The following pamphlets are published by the Public Affairs Committee, 22 East 38th Street, New York, New York.

Black, Algernon D. *If I Marry Outside My Religion*. Pamphlet No. 204.

Carson, Ruth. *Having a Baby*. Pamphlet No. 178.

Duvall, Evelyn Millis. *Building Your Marriage*. Pamphlet No. 113.

Duvall, Evelyn Millis. *Keeping Up with Teen-Agers*. Pamphlet No. 127.

Duvall, Evelyn and Sylvanus. *Saving Your Marriage*. Pamphlet No. 213.

Eckert, Ralph G. *So You Think It's Love*. Pamphlet No. 161.

Hymes, James L. *How to Tell Your Child About Sex*. Pamphlet No. 149.

Kirkendall, Lester A. *Too Young to Marry*. Pamphlet No. 236.

Landis, Paul H. *Coming of Age: Problems of Teen-Agers*. Pamphlet No. 234.

Neisser, Edith G. *Mother-in-law and Grandmother*. Pamphlet No. 174.

Ogg, Elizabeth. *When Parents Grow Old*. Pamphlet No. 208.

Osborne, Ernest. *Democracy Begins in the Home*. Pamphlet No. 192.

Osborne, Ernest. *How to Teach Your Child About Work*. Pamphlet No. 216.

Polier, Justine Wise. *Back to What Woodshed?* Pamphlet No. 232.

Thorman, George. *Broken Homes*. Pamphlet No. 135.

NOTE: The following Life Adjustment Booklets are published by Science Research Associates, 57 West Grand Avenue, Chicago, Illinois.

Adams, Clifford R. *Looking Ahead to Marriage*.

Bauer, William W., and Donald A. Dukelow. *What You Should Know About Smoking and Drinking*.

Bouthilet, Lorraine, and Katherine M. Byrne. *You and Your Mental Abilities.*

Cosgrove, Marjorie, and Irma Unrush. *Discovering Yourself,* 1957.

Eckert, Ralph G. *What You Should Know About Parenthood.*

English, Spurgeon O., and Constance J. Foster. *Your Behavior Problems.*

Gallagher, J. Roswell. *You and Your Health.*

Henry, William E. *Exploring Your Personality.*

Hertz, Barbara V. *Where Are Your Manners?*

Humphreys, Anthony J. *Choosing Your Career.*

Jenkins, Gladys G., and Joy Neuman. *How to Live with Parents.*

Kirkendall, Lester A. *Understanding Sex.*

Kirkendall, Lester A., and Ruth F. Osborne. *Dating Days.*

Kirkendall, Lester A., and Ruth F. Osborne. *Understanding the Other Sex.*

Kuder, Frederick G., and Blanche B. Paulson. *Discovering Your Real Interests.*

Lasser, J. K., and Sylvia F. Porter. *Money and You.*

Menninger, William C. *Enjoying Leisure Time.*

Menninger, William C. *Making and Keeping Friends.*

Menninger, William C. *Understanding Yourself.*

Remmers, H. H. *What Are Your Problems?*

Seashore, Robert H., and A. C. Van Dusen. *How to Solve Your Problems.*

Shacter, Helen. *Getting Along with Others.*

Shanner, William. *A Guide to Logical Thinking.*

Stevens, Patricia. *A Guide to Good Grooming.*

Taylor, Florence. *Why Stay in School?*

Taylor, Katharine Whiteside. *Getting Along with Parents.*

Ullmann, Frances. *Getting Along with Brothers and Sisters.*

Weitzman, Ellis. *Growing Up Socially.*

Wrenn, Gilbert C. *How to Increase Your Self-Confidence.*

NOTE: The following pamphlets are prepared for the Joint Committee on Health Problems in Education of the National Education Association and the American Medical Association. They are distributed by: National Education Association, 1201 Sixteenth Street, N. W., Washington, D. C., or American Medical Association, 535 N. Dearborn Street, Chicago, Illinois.

Learning About Love. (Ages 16 to 20), 1955.

Facts Aren't Enough. (Adults), 1955.

Finding Yourself. (Ages 12 to 15), 1955.

Duvall, Evelyn Millis, and Reuben Hill. *When You Marry.* D. C. Heath and Company, Boston, 1953.

The Adolescent in Your Family. Publication No. 347, U. S. Department of Health, Education, and Welfare, 1954.

REFERENCES

Craig, Hazel Thompson. *Thresholds to Adult Living*. Peoria, Ill.: Charles A. Bennett Company, Inc., 1962.

Duvall, Evelyn Millis, and Reuben Hill. *Being Married*. New York: Association Press, 1960.

——. *When You Marry* (High School Edition). Boston: D. C. Heath and Company, 1962.

——. *Personal Adjustment, Marriage and Family Living*. Englewood Cliffs, N. J.: Prentice-Hall, Inc., 1960.

Feldman, Frances Lomas. *The Family in a Money World*. Family Service Association of America, 1957.

Landis, Judson T., and Mary G. Landis. *Building a Successful Marriage*, 3d ed. Englewood Cliffs, N. J.: Prentice-Hall, Inc., 1958.

Osborne, Ernest G. *Understanding Your Parents*. New York: Association Press, 1956.

Peterson, James A. *Education for Marriage*. New York: Charles Scribner's Sons, 1956.

Scheinfeld, Amram. *The Basic Facts of Human Heredity*. New York: Washington Square Press, Inc., 1961.

Strain, Frances Bruce. *Sex Guidance in Family Life Education*. New York: The Macmillan Co., 1948.

Thomas (S. J.), John L. *The American Catholic Family*. Englewood Cliffs, N. J.: Prentice-Hall, Inc., 1956.

The Pastor's Companion. St. Louis: Concordia Publishing House, 1953.

PAMPHLETS

Girls Want to Know, Boys Want to Know, Preparing for Your Marriage. American Social Hygiene Association, 1952.

Sweeney, Ester Emerson. *Dates and Dating*. American Social Hygiene Assn. 5th Printing, 1956. Copyright. YWCA, 1948.

Neisser, Edith G. *The Many Faces of Money*. Human Relations Aids, New York, N. Y.

Christian Guidance on Marriage and Family Life. The Board of Social Missions of the United Lutheran Church in America, 1956.